Jewish
REGIONAL COOKING

RICHARD HAASE
Jewish
REGIONAL COOKING

CHARTWELL
BOOKS, INC.

A QUARTO BOOK

ISBN 0 89009 943 X

This book was designed and produced by
Quarto Publishing Ltd
The Old Brewery, 6 Blundell Street, London N7 9BH

Senior Editor Jane Rollason
Designer Peter Bridgewater
Illustrator Lorraine Harrison
Food photography Edward Hing, Janine Norton
Art Editor Moira Clinch

Art Director Alastair Campbell
Editorial Director Jim Miles

Typeset by QV Typesetting Ltd, London
Color origination by Rainbow Graphic Arts Co Ltd, Hong Kong
Printed by LeeFung-Asco Printers Ltd, Hong Kong

*Dedicated to the memory of my uncles Thomas
and James Bosco without whose love and
guidance I might not be a writer today.*

Contents

The diaspora of Jewish culture

The word diaspora comes from the Greek word meaning scattering. It generally refers to the scattering of the Jewish people outside of Israel, a process with ancient origins.

Forty years after their flight from Egypt under the leadership of Moses, the Jews arrived at the promised land of Canaan. Under the leadership of Joshua, they conquered Canaan and established themselves there. By the time of Solomon, about 970 BCE, the Jews had become a cohesive society centered in Israel. Even then, however, Jews lived outside the homeland, in Egypt and elsewhere.

After the Assyrian conquests of Israel in 722 BCE many Jews were dispersed to the east into Persia and the area near the Caspian Sea. The first catastrophic exile of the Jews occurred when Judea fell to the Babylonians and the Temple in Jerusalem was destroyed in 586 BCE. The Jews were exiled from their homeland, with many carried off into captivity in Babylonia. In Babylon they enjoyed a surprising level of prosperity and religious freedom, but still yearned for Israel. The desire to return was fulfilled in 539 BCE, when Babylonia was in turn conquered by Cyrus the Great, King of the Persians. Cyrus, the founder of the Persian Empire, issued a proclamation allowing the Jews to return to their homeland and permitting them to rebuild the Temple. (The new Temple was dedicated in 516 BCE.) Many Jews returned, although many others stayed on in Babylonia and made it an important center of Jewish culture. By this time there were also significant Jewish communities in Syria, Egypt and Persia.

The Persian Empire lasted until the advent of Alexander the Great. By the time of Alexander's death in 323 BCE, much that had been Persian was now part of his enormous empire.

The Hellenization of the Middle East, which began with Alexander and continued for seven centuries, had enormous significance for the Jews. Greek language, art, philosophy, religion and culture were important influences, particularly for those Jews living outside the Holy Land. The city of Alexandria, founded by Alexander in 332 BCE, was a major center of Jewish culture for centuries. The Jews there held important positions in the Greek and later in the Roman world. Their synagogue was famed for its beauty.

Foreign rule and foreign religions were less congenial to the Jews still living in Palestine. In the middle of the second century BCE the Jews, under the leadership of Judas Maccabeus, revolted against the despotic rule of Antiochus and established an independent Jewish state in 165 BCE. The victory and the miraculous rededication of the Temple that followed are commemorated on the holiday of Chanuka.

The Hasmonean dynasty founded by Judas was conquered by the Romans in 63 BCE. This brought further dispersal of the Jews from their homeland, but now the dispersal was not so much eastward towards Persia (although Jews reached Bombay by 175 BCE) but westward into Roman Europe, particularly to Rome and Italy. From there, Jews settled in Spain and France, and then in England and Germany. Persecution in Germany forced them into Poland and Russia.

By 750 CE, the Islamic conquest of the Mediterranean was well underway. The Muslims were far more tolerant of the Jews than the Christians were, and Jewish communities flourished in Spain, North Africa and the Middle East. Nonetheless, the Jews still faced discrimination and persecution, conditions that persist into this century in Muslim countries.

The expulsion of the Jews from Spain and Portugal in the fifteenth century scattered them further. Some settled in North Africa, while others went to Amsterdam, Turkey and the New World.

The scattering of the Jews continued over the centuries. It was accelerated once again starting in the 1880s by persecution and political instability in Russia and Eastern Europe. Many Jews emigrated to Western Europe and America at this time.

World War I led to massive dislocations of the Jews and large-scale emigration to America and elsewhere. The Holocaust of World War II virtually destroyed the Jewish communities of Europe. Many of the Jews who survived Nazi rule were dispersed to America and to the new state of Israel.

ISRAEL & THE ISLAMIC WORLD	FRANCE & ITALY
RUSSIA & EASTERN EUROPE	SPAIN, PORTUGAL & THE NEW WORLD
GERMANY & AUSTRIA	ENGLISH-SPEAKING WORLD

Because of the diaspora of Jewish culture, there is no one style of Jewish cooking. The Jews, wherever they were, adapted the local cuisine to their dietary laws. The diversity of Jewish culture is reflected in the many Jewish cooking styles from different lands.

The modern kosher kitchen

Jewish cooking is based on the observance of the dietary laws set forth in the Bible and elaborated by rabbinical ordinances.

The laws divide food into permitted and forbidden categories. The permitted foods are popularly called 'kosher', from the Hebrew *kasher*, and the forbidden foods are called 'trayf', from the Hebrew *terefah*.

For meats to be kosher, they must come from an animal that has a cloven hoof, that chews the cud and that has been ritually slaughtered. This means that beef, lamb, veal and even goat are kosher, but that rabbit, for example, is not. Pork is strictly forbidden. Among birds, ritually slaughtered barnyard poultry are generally kosher, but birds of prey and scavengers are not. Seafood must have fins and scales. Eels, shellfish and crustaceans are not kosher. (Whether the sturgeon, which technically has bony plates, not scales, is kosher is debatable.) Insects and reptiles are not kosher.

The blood of animals must not be eaten, and all meat must be well drained and salted before using, which is why liver is always cooked very thoroughly in Jewish cooking. Animals are slaughtered by a *shochet*, who must be a pious man learned in the law. It is his obligation to kill the animal instantly and humanely and to inspect it for disease. The sciatic nerve, found in the hindquarter of the animal, is forbidden. It can be removed by a kosher butcher, but in practice only the forequarters of the animal are generally sold as kosher meat and the hindquarters are sold to a non-kosher butcher.

An important part of the dietary laws is the prohibition against mixing milk ('milchig') foods and meat ('fleischig') foods. This dates back to the Biblical injunction against cooking a kid in its mother's milk. Jewish cooking is filled with ingenious ways of complying with this prohibition. In modern times, the development of non-dairy cream

KOSHER WINES

KOSHER MEATS

SOYA MILK & YOGHURT

MATZOHS & BAGELS

substitute, soybean-based ice-cream and artificial bacon bits has been a boon to kosher cooks. To avoid contaminating one food with the other, observant households maintain two separate sets of dishes and cooking utensils, one for meat meals and the other for dairy. Foods such as fruits, vegetables, spices, coffee and tea, fish and eggs are considered 'pareve' or neutral. They may be used with meat or milk, although vegetables for a meat meal should be prepared with the meat utensils. The same applies to dairy meals. Meat and dairy foods should not follow directly after each other; there should be an interval.

The Sabbath and holidays are traditionally ushered in by the *kiddush*, a traditional benediction over wine or bread. Kosher grape wine should be used for the kiddush. A wine is kosher if the grapes have been grown and the wine made by observant Jews. Kosher wines are generally thought of as heavy and sweet, but many excellent drier, lighter wines are now available.

The interpretation of the kosher laws varies somewhat from country to country. Many observant Italian Jews, for example, do not keep two sets of dishes. All of the recipes in this collection follow kosher dietary laws, although many of them have had to be adapted to do so. If you are in doubt about the dietary laws, any rabbi will be happy to answer your questions.

The menus assembled here try to follow the authentic eating patterns of the countries from which they derive. It is important to remember that, sadly, many of these menus are historical, dating from before World War II. The societies that developed them are largely non-existent now. Calorie and cholesterol-counting were unknown then, as were the dangers of too much salt in the diet. Although the individual recipes here have been modernized to conform to today's ideas of good eating, the overall effect of some of the menus may still be too heavy for some.

The traditional Yiddish for *bon appetit* is *ess gesindeheit*, meaning roughly, 'eat in good health'. The traditional Yiddish toast is *l'chaim*, or 'to life'. In Hebrew, *bon appetit* is *bete-avon* and the toast is *lehitraot*, or cheers.

Israel
and the Islamic World

Israel Since the founding of Israel in 1948, Jews from all over the world have come to live there. Many were refugees from Hitler's Europe, but many also came from the oppressed communities of Iran, Iraq, Saudi Arabia, Yemen and North Africa.

Israeli cooking combines elements from both European and Middle Eastern styles, with a strong emphasis on native fruits and vegetables and not very much meat. Many dishes that are widely thought to be Israeli, such as falafel and hummus, in fact originated in Arab countries.

The Middle East The earliest Jewish cuisine originated in the Middle East. Both Islamic and Jewish law forbid the consumption of pork, and Muslims and Jews tend to have a similar diet. The Middle Eastern style of cooking is largely vegetarian and dairy, and uses many herbs and spices. A dish is considered successful if it has a sharp and pronounced contrast of flavors. Among the most popular spices are coriander, turmeric and cardamom. Chicken and lamb are virtually the only meats used. Other important dishes are lentils, bread and couscous.

North Africa Jewish trading communities flourished all along the North African coast from the fifth century BCE to the period of the Islamic conquests in the eighth century CE. During Roman times, as many as six million Jews lived in this thriving area, including nearly a million Jews in Alexandria alone. Their numbers dwindled after Muslim rule was imposed, but were boosted by an influx of Spanish and Portuguese Jews fleeing the Inquisition in the fifteenth century. The Jews of Libya, Algeria, Egypt, Tunisia and Morocco were subject to continuous persecution in the centuries that followed. The Egyptian community, although diminished in size, remained important. The Jews elsewhere in North Africa gradually became trapped in impoverished ghettos.

After 1948, emigration to Israel from North Africa was massive. Fewer than one thousand Jews today remain in Egypt. Of the thirty thousand Jews who lived in Libya before World War II, virtually none remain. The populations of Morocco and Tunisia today are a tenth of their size in 1960.

The North African Jews have a distinct culture. The Tunisian Jews, for example, speak Arabic and have their own rituals. In modern-day Israel, the North African Jews have been largely assimilated, but still maintain many of their unique characteristics.

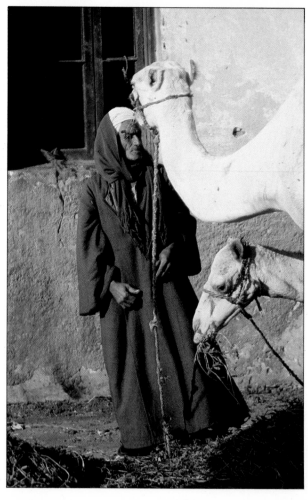

The religious, ritual and culinary aspects of Jewish life are richly interwoven.

Honey Cake ABOVE is a classic Jewish dessert
served around the world (page 20).

◆

Tomato Salad with Olives BELOW adds a Middle
Eastern flavor to any main course (page 24).

Baked Perch ABOVE *is a delightfully simple main
course for a dairy meal (page 27).*

◆

Lamb and Okra Stew BELOW *is a classic dish of
Egyptian-Jewish cuisine (page 31).*

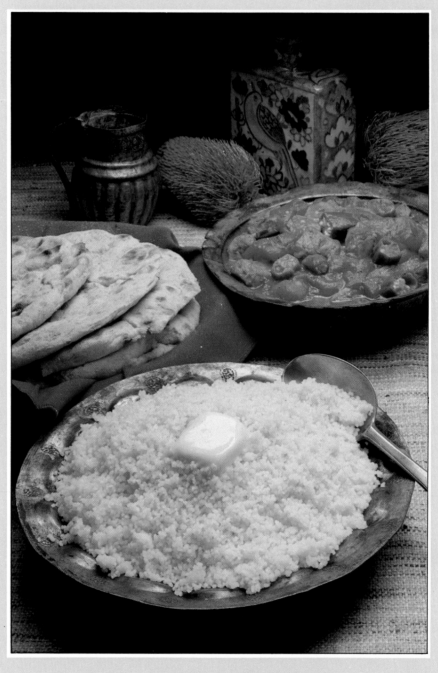

*Couscous, a staple dish throughout North Africa,
makes an interesting alternative to rice or pasta
(page 31).*

Israeli Dairy Lunch

Israel is a melting pot for Jews from many nations. In that sense, there really is little in the way of native Israeli cuisine. However, the Israelis have made the desert bloom, and the use of fresh fruits and vegetables is characteristic of their cooking.

Melon Appetizer
Sinai Jellied Fish
Zucchini Soufflé
Stuffed Pears
Honey Cake

Melon Appetizer

SERVES 6

This delicious first course takes an ordinary melon and turns it into something special.

3 oranges, peeled, seeded and sectioned

1 large pink grapefruit, peeled, seeded and sectioned

6 tablespoons Triple Sec or other orange-flavored liqueur

3 tablespoons grenadine syrup

1 cup fresh pomegranate seeds

3 teaspoons finely chopped fresh mint

3 small cantaloupes, halved and seeded

In a small mixing bowl, combine the orange and grapefruit sections, Triple Sec, grenadine syrup, pomegranate seeds and mint. Refrigerate for 1 hour.
♦ Spoon the fruit mixture evenly into the cantaloupe halves.

Sinai Jellied Fish

SERVES 6

This cold fish dish is of Eastern European ancestry. Any firm white fish fillets may be used.

2 pounds fish heads and trimmings

2 cups water

1 cup white wine

1 celery stalk, diced

1 bay leaf

$\frac{1}{2}$ cup coarsely chopped parsley

2 onions, quartered

$\frac{1}{2}$ teaspoon black pepper

2 tablespoons lemon juice

$\frac{1}{4}$ teaspoon salt

2 tablespoons olive oil

2 pounds fish fillets

Place all the ingredients except the fish fillets in a medium-sized saucepan. Bring the liquid to a boil over high heat. Reduce the heat to medium, cover, and cook for 1 hour.
♦ Strain the fish broth through a fine sieve into another saucepan. Discard any solids remaining in the sieve. Add the fish fillets to the fish broth, cover, and simmer over low heat for 20 minutes.
♦ Carefully remove the fish fillets and place them in a deep dish. Pour the broth over the fish and chill until the broth jellies. Serve cold.

Zucchini Soufflé

SERVES 6

French flair combines with a Middle Eastern influence to create this unusual and delicious soufflé.

¼ cup butter

½ cup finely chopped onion

¼ cup flour

1 cup milk

1 tablespoon grated Parmesan cheese

½ cup feta cheese, crumbled

2½ cups zucchini, finely chopped

¼ teaspoon salt

¼ teaspoon black pepper

4 egg yolks

5 egg whites

Preheat the oven to 350°F. Melt the butter in a large saucepan over a medium heat. Add the onion and sauté for 2 minutes. Add the flour and cook for an additional 2 minutes.

♦ Add the milk and cook, stirring constantly, until the milk begins to bubble and thicken. Add the Parmesan and feta cheese and stir until well mixed.

♦ Add the zucchini, salt and pepper. Reduce the heat to low and cook for 1 minute.

♦ Stir in the yolks one at a time. When all the egg yolks are blended, remove the saucepan from the heat.

♦ In a small mixing bowl, beat the egg whites until they are stiff. Fold the egg whites into the zucchini soufflé mixture. Pour the mixture into a buttered soufflé dish. Bake for 45 minutes, or until the soufflé is puffed and browned. Serve at once.

Stuffed Pears

SERVES 6

This recipe uses dates and walnuts to create a simple and delightful dessert.

¼ cup dates, pitted and chopped

½ cup ground walnuts

½ teaspoon cinnamon

12 canned pear halves, drained

½ cup water

½ cup sugar

1 cup white wine

2 whole cloves

2 tablespoons lemon juice

Preheat the oven to 350°F. In a small mixing bowl, combine the dates, walnuts and cinnamon. Mix well. Fill the cavities of the pear halves with the mixture. Place the pears in a shallow baking dish.

♦ In a small saucepan, bring the water, sugar, wine, cloves and lemon juice to a boil over a medium heat. Stir frequently until the sugar is dissolved. Reduce the heat to low and simmer for 2 minutes.

♦ Pour the wine sauce over the pears in the baking dish. Bake for 20 minutes. Chill for 1 hour before serving.

Honey Cake

SERVES 6—8

A classic Jewish dessert all over the world, honey cake is traditionally served on the Sabbath and festivals. In Israel, it is served all year round.

$\frac{1}{4}$ cup plus 1 teaspoon vegetable oil

$2\frac{1}{4}$ cups flour

$\frac{1}{4}$ cup seedless golden raisins

$\frac{1}{4}$ cup chopped candied orange peel

3 eggs, separated

1 cup honey

$\frac{1}{4}$ cup sugar

2 teaspoons finely grated lemon rind

4 teaspoons instant coffee dissolved in $1\frac{1}{2}$ tablespoons boiling water

1 teaspoon baking powder

$\frac{1}{4}$ teaspoon baking soda

$\frac{1}{4}$ teaspoon pure vanilla extract

$\frac{1}{4}$ teaspoon cinnamon

$\frac{1}{4}$ teaspoon ground allspice

$\frac{1}{4}$ teaspoon salt

$\frac{1}{2}$ cup blanched almonds, sliced

Preheat the oven to 325°F. Coat a 9×5×3 inch baking pan with 1 teaspoon of the vegetable oil. Dust the pan lightly with $1\frac{1}{2}$ tablespoons of flour and set aside.

♦ Combine the raisins, candied orange peel, and 2 tablespoons flour in a small mixing bowl. Mix together until the fruit is evenly coated with the flour and set aside.

♦ In another mixing bowl, beat the egg yolks until they begin to froth. Beat in the remaining oil, honey, sugar, lemon rind and concentrated coffee mixture. Gradually beat in the remaining flour, baking powder, baking soda, vanilla extract, cinnamon, allspice and salt. Continue beating until the mixture is smooth. Stir in the raisins and orange peel.

♦ In a small mixing bowl, beat the egg whites until they are stiff. Gently fold the egg whites into the batter. Pour the batter into the greased baking pan and top with the almonds. Bake for 1 hour 15 minutes. Cool at room temperature.

Israeli Sabbath Meal

This Sabbath meal is an exotic departure from the traditional fare of Jews whose roots are in German-speaking countries and Eastern Europe. Challah would be served with the meal.

Stuffed Dates
Pickled Lemons
Avocado Soup
Chicken with Kumquats
Tomato Salad with Olives
Orange Pudding

Stuffed Dates

SERVES 6 — 8

This dish of stuffed dates on ground veal patties should be served with pickled lemons (see below).

1 tablespoon margarine

1 pound ground veal

$\frac{1}{4}$ teaspoon thyme

$\frac{1}{4}$ cup melted margarine

32 unsalted roasted almonds

32 dried dates, pitted

Melt the margarine in a small skillet. Add the veal and thyme and cook over a low heat for 15 minutes, or until the veal is thoroughly browned. Drain off any fat that has accumulated in the skillet. Set the veal aside.

♦ Preheat the oven to 375°F. When the veal is cool enough to handle, form it into 32 thin patties each with a diameter of about 1 inch. Place the patties on a greased baking sheet.

♦ Insert an almond into each date. Top each veal patty with a stuffed date. Pour the melted margarine over the patties and bake for 10 minutes. Serve hot.

Pickled Lemons

MAKES 2 to 3 PINTS

Israel is famous for citrus fruits. Make these lemon pickles three weeks in advance.

12 lemons, thinly sliced and seeded

$\frac{1}{4}$ cup salt

3 teaspoons paprika

1 teaspoon black peppercorns

2 bay leaves

$1\frac{1}{2}$ cups corn oil

$\frac{1}{2}$ cup olive oil

Arrange the lemon slices in layers in a colander, sprinkling the salt between the layers. Leave them to stand for 24 hours.

♦ Place the lemon slices in a mixing bowl and sprinkle them with the paprika. Divide the lemon slices among two 1 pint sterilized glass jars. Add $\frac{1}{2}$ teaspoon of the peppercorns and 1 bay leaf to each jar.

♦ Mix the oils together in a bowl. Fill each jar with the oil mixture, making sure that no air bubbles are trapped in the jars. Seal the jars tightly and store them in the refrigerator for 3 weeks before serving.

Avocado Soup

SERVES 6

Similar to pea soup in texture, avocado soup has a delightful nutty flavor.

4 tablespoons margarine

1 cup finely chopped onion

3 tablespoons flour

5 cups chicken broth

2 ripe avocados

2 egg yolks

2 tablespoons lemon juice

$\frac{1}{2}$ teaspoon salt

$\frac{1}{2}$ teaspoon white pepper

Melt the margarine in a small saucepan over a low heat. Add the onions and sauté for 2 minutes. Sprinkle the onions with the flour and sauté for 3 to 5 minutes longer. Add 1 cup of the chicken broth and bring the mixture to a boil, stirring frequently.

◆ Pour the onion and broth mixture into a large saucepan. Add the remaining broth and bring the mixture to a boil over a medium heat, stirring frequently. Reduce the heat to very low and simmer, covered, for 5 minutes.

◆ Halve the avocados and remove the pits. Peel the avocado halves and mash the pulp in a bowl. Add the egg yolks, lemon juice, salt and pepper to the bowl and blend well.

◆ Stir the avocado mixture into the soup and cook gently for 3 to 5 minutes. Do not let the soup boil. Serve hot.

Chicken with Kumquats

SERVES 6

This chicken dish has a definite Middle Eastern tang.

2 × 3 pound chickens, cut into pieces

$1\frac{1}{2}$ cups orange juice

$\frac{1}{4}$ cup apricot preserves

$\frac{1}{4}$ cup peach preserves

$\frac{1}{4}$ cup honey

1 teaspoon cayenne pepper

$\frac{1}{4}$ cup lemon juice

2 cups canned kumquats, drained

Preheat the oven to 400°F. Arrange the chicken pieces in a large, lightly greased baking dish and bake for 30 minutes.

◆ Combine the orange juice, apricot preserves, peach preserves, honey, cayenne pepper and lemon juice in a mixing bowl. Mix well.

◆ After the chicken has baked for 30 minutes, brush the pieces with half the orange juice mixture. Reduce the oven temperature to 350°F and bake for 15 minutes.

◆ Turn the chicken pieces over and brush them with the remaining orange juice mixture. Arrange the kumquats in the pan with the chicken. Bake for 15 minutes longer. Pour the pan juices over the chicken and kumquats before serving.

Tomato Salad with Olives

SERVES 6

A crispy contrast to chicken with kumquats (see p.23), this salad is best when made with imported Middle Eastern-style olives.

4 large ripe tomatoes, thinly sliced

2 cucumbers, peeled and thinly sliced

1 cup black olives, pitted

For the dressing:

2 tablespoons finely chopped parsley

1 tablespoon finely chopped mint

$\frac{1}{4}$ cup lemon juice

2 tablespoons tarragon vinegar

$\frac{1}{4}$ cup olive oil

$\frac{1}{4}$ teaspoon salt

$\frac{1}{2}$ teaspoon black pepper

Arrange the tomato and cucumber slices on a serving platter. Arrange the olives around the cucumbers and tomatoes.

♦ To make the dressing, combine the parsley, mint, lemon juice, vinegar, oil, salt and pepper in a small bowl. Mix well with a fork or small whisk until well blended. Pour the dressing over the salad. Chill for 30 minutes and serve cold.

Orange Pudding

SERVES 6

A welcome change from the usual pudding flavors, this recipe has the added advantage of being pareve.

rind from 2 oranges, finely grated

1 cup sugar

$\frac{2}{3}$ cup cornstarch

$\frac{1}{4}$ teaspoon salt

4 eggs, separated

5 cups orange juice

In a large mixing bowl combine the orange rind, sugar, cornstarch and salt.

♦ In a separate bowl beat the egg yolks into the orange juice. Gradually add the cornstarch mixture and stir until smooth.

♦ Put the mixture into a medium-sized saucepan. Cook over a medium heat, stirring constantly, until the custard mixture thickens, about 12 minutes.

♦ Remove the saucepan from the heat and plunge it into a large pan of cold water. Leave it for 2 to 3 minutes.

♦ Beat the egg whites in a small mixing bowl until they are stiff. Fold the egg whites into the custard until the mixture is smooth. Spoon the pudding into tulip glasses or dessert dishes and chill before serving.

Israeli Dairy Lunch

This traditional dairy lunch includes a baked perch dish that is hundreds of years old.

Fruit Soup
Avocado with Honey Sauce
Baked Perch
Horseradish Condiment
Braised Carrots and Oranges
Almond Loaf

♦

Fruit Soup

SERVES 6

This fruit soup can be made with nearly any fruit in season. It was probably brought to Israel by Jews from Slavic countries.

2 ripe peaches, halved and pitted

4 ripe plums, halved and pitted

3 ripe apricots, halved and pitted

2 apples, peeled, cored and halved

1 cup strawberries

$\frac{1}{2}$ cup ripe cherries, pitted

$\frac{1}{4}$ cup lemon juice

4 cups water

$\frac{1}{2}$ cup sugar

1 cup white wine

$1\frac{1}{2}$ cups soured cream

Place the fruits, lemon juice, water and sugar in a large pot. Simmer, covered, over a medium heat for 25 minutes.

♦ Turn the heat off. Mash the fruits with a fork into a thick paste. Add the wine. Simmer over a low heat for 5 minutes.

♦ Serve cold, adding a dollop of soured cream to each bowl of soup just before serving.

Avocado with Honey Sauce

SERVES 6—8

The sweetness of the honey, the naturally nutty flavor of the avocado and the citrus tang of the grapefruit make this an interesting appetizer.

1 onion, finely chopped

1 teaspoon dry mustard

$\frac{1}{2}$ cup honey

$\frac{1}{2}$ cup lemon juice

$\frac{1}{2}$ cup olive oil

4 large avocados

1 large grapefruit, peeled, seeded and sectioned

In a large mixing bowl, combine the onion, mustard, honey, lemon juice and olive oil. Mix thoroughly. Chill the honey sauce for 30 minutes.

♦ Halve the avocados and remove the pits. Cut each avocado half into wedges approximately the same size as the grapefruit sections. Remove the outer skin. Arrange the avocado wedges alternately with grapefruit sections in small dishes. Spoon some of the honey sauce over each portion and serve.

Baked Perch

SERVES 6—8

This recipe is traditionally made with mushat, a fish native to the Sea of Galilee.
Perch is a good substitute.

8 large perch fillets

$\frac{1}{4}$ teaspoon salt

$\frac{1}{4}$ teaspoon black pepper

1 cup coarsely chopped onion

3 tablespoons coarsely chopped parsley

$\frac{1}{2}$ cup white wine

$\frac{1}{4}$ cup lemon juice

$\frac{1}{4}$ cup olive oil

Preheat the oven to 375°F. In a large baking pan, arrange the perch fillets skin-side down. Sprinkle with the salt and pepper and top with the onion.
♦ Combine the parsley, wine, lemon juice and olive oil in a small mixing bowl. Mix thoroughly.
♦ Pour half the olive oil mixture over the fish and bake for 10 minutes. Baste the fish with the remaining olive oil mixture and bake for 10 minutes longer. Serve immediately.

Horseradish Condiment

MAKES 1$\frac{1}{2}$ CUPS

3 beets, peeled

$\frac{1}{2}$ cup finely grated fresh white horseradish root

$\frac{1}{4}$ teaspoon black pepper

2$\frac{1}{2}$ tablespoons sugar

1$\frac{1}{2}$ cups white vinegar

Cook the beets in a large, covered pot of boiling water over a medium heat for 40 minutes. Drain well and chill the beets for 30 minutes.
♦ Finely grate or chop the beets.
♦ Combine the horseradish, grated beet, pepper, sugar and vinegar in a mixing bowl. Mix thoroughly until well blended. Chill and serve with hot or cold fish.

Braised Carrots and Oranges

SERVES 6—8

This side dish goes very well with fish and chicken dishes.

2 pounds baby carrots, peeled

1 cup chopped onion

$\frac{1}{4}$ cup olive oil

1 cup water

2 tablespoons sugar

2 teaspoons lemon juice

$\frac{1}{4}$ teaspoon salt

$\frac{1}{4}$ teaspoon black pepper

$1\frac{1}{2}$ cups drained, canned mandarin orange sections

$\frac{1}{4}$ cup orange juice

Combine all the ingredients in a medium-sized saucepan. Simmer, uncovered, over a low heat for 15 minutes, stirring frequently. Cover the saucepan and simmer for an additional 5 to 10 minutes, or until the carrots are tender. Serve warm.

Almond Loaf

MAKES 1 LOAF

A deliciously light dessert, almond loaf is also wonderful with morning coffee or afternoon tea.

4 eggs

1 cup sugar

$\frac{1}{4}$ teaspoon pure almond extract

1 teaspoon baking powder

$\frac{1}{4}$ teaspoon salt

$\frac{1}{2}$ teaspoon ground cinnamon

1 cup flour

1 tablespoon melted margarine

$1\frac{1}{2}$ cups finely chopped unsalted, roasted almonds

Preheat the oven to 350°F. Lightly grease a 9 inch loaf pan.

♦ Beat the eggs in a mixing bowl. Gradually beat in the sugar. Add the almond extract, baking powder, salt and cinnamon. Add the flour, melted margarine and almonds. Stir until the batter is well blended. Pour the batter into the loaf pan and bake for 40 minutes.

♦ Invert the pan over a cooling rack and turn the loaf out. Let the almond loaf cool. When it is cool, cut it into quarters. Cut the quarters into $\frac{1}{2}$ inch slices. Re-form the slices into a loaf shape in the pan and bake at 325°F for 10 minutes. Turn off the heat and leave the loaf in the oven for 15 minutes.

Egyptian Jewish Supper

There have been Jews in Egypt for over five thousand years, since long before the pyramids were built. Egyptian-Jewish cuisine developed over the centuries from a means of sustenance into a sophisticated art. It bears some close resemblances to its Muslim and Coptic Christian counterparts.

Bean Patties

Garlic Sauce

Lamb and Okra Stew

Couscous

Mazza

Semolina Cake

Bean Patties

SERVES 6

Egyptian cuisine makes heavy use of beans and legumes. Serve these bean patties with garlic sauce (see below). These patties can be served as a meal on their own, accompanied by salad, rice and pita bread.

3 cups dried broad beans

1½ cups finely chopped onions

½ cup finely chopped parsley

2 tablespoons finely chopped fresh coriander

5 garlic cloves, minced

1 teaspoon salt

¼ teaspoon black pepper

¼ teaspoon cayenne pepper

½ teaspoon baking soda

3 teaspoons sesame seeds

2 cups vegetable oil

Put the beans into a large bowl and add 9 cups of cold water. Soak the beans for 48 hours, changing the water every 12 hours.

♦ Drain the beans. Squeeze the beans between the fingers to pop off the skins. Discard the skins.

♦ In a large mixing bowl, mash the beans with the onions, parsley, coriander, garlic, salt, black pepper, cayenne pepper and baking soda. Mash until smooth.

♦ Shape the bean mixture into small, round patties about 1 inch in diameter. Sprinkle sesame seeds over both sides of each patty, gently pressing the seeds into the patties.

♦ Heat the vegetable oil in a large, heavy skillet over a medium heat until it is very hot. Add as many bean patties as will fit in a single layer. Cook the patties for 3 minutes on each side.

Garlic Sauce

MAKES ½ CUP

Serve the garlic sauce in a small dish along with the bean patties. This garlic sauce also goes well with roast lamb or baked fish.

6 garlic cloves, finely chopped

¼ teaspoon salt

4 tablespoons clarified margarine or butter

1 teaspoon ground coriander

¼ teaspoon cayenne pepper

Combine all the ingredients in a small saucepan and cook for 2 minutes over a low heat.

Lamb and Okra Stew

SERVES 6

The okra in this stew gives it a natural thickness and savory taste. Be careful not to overcook the okra, or it will become stringy. Serve the stew with couscous (see below).

3 tablespoons margarine

$2\frac{1}{2}$ pounds boneless stewing lamb, cubed

1 cup chopped onion

1 teaspoon ground cumin

1 cup canned tomatoes

4 tablespoons tomato paste

$1\frac{1}{2}$ cups chicken broth

$\frac{1}{2}$ teaspoon salt

$\frac{1}{2}$ teaspoon black pepper

$\frac{1}{2}$ teaspoon sugar

1 pound fresh okra

$\frac{1}{2}$ cup water

$\frac{1}{2}$ cup white vinegar

Melt 2 tablespoons of the margarine in a large skillet. Add the lamb cubes and sauté until they are browned on all sides. Add the onion, cumin, tomatoes, tomato paste, chicken broth, salt, pepper and sugar to the skillet. Cook over a low heat, stirring frequently, for 5 minutes.

♦ Preheat the oven to 325°F. Transfer the lamb mixture from the skillet to a medium-sized casserole. Cover the dish and bake for 90 minutes.

♦ Trim the okra and cut it into thin slices. Soak the slices in the water and vinegar for 20 minutes. Drain and pat the okra dry with paper towels.

♦ Melt the remaining margarine in a small skillet. Add the okra slices and sauté for 6 minutes, stirring frequently.

♦ After the casserole has baked for 90 minutes, add the okra slices to it. Stir well, cover the dish, and bake for a further 40 minutes. Serve hot.

Couscous

SERVES 6

Couscous is made from a fine wheat semolina. It is a staple dish throughout all of North Africa. Ideally, couscous should be steamed in a large copper couscousier or prepared as described here.

4 cups couscous

1 cup cold water

1 cup flour

1 teaspoon salt

Place the couscous on a large flat plate and shape it into a mound with an indentation in the center. Fill the indentation with 1 cup cold water. Using fingers, gradually work the water through the couscous, moistening it evenly.

♦ Mix the flour with the salt in a bowl. Gradually sprinkle the flour mixture over the couscous, working it in until all the couscous is coated with flour.

♦ Press the floured couscous through a medium sieve. Put it in a metal colander lined with cheesecloth. Place the colander in a pot large enough to hold it. Add enough water to the pot to cover the base or legs of the colander. Cover the pot tightly and steam the couscous for 12 minutes. Break up any lumps with your fingers.

Mazza

SERVES 6

One translation of 'mazza' might be tahini salad, but it is not a salad in the conventional sense of the word. Mazza should be served in small bowls with the main course. It is nibbled in small bites to cleanse the palate. Tahini or sesame seed paste is available in Middle Eastern and well-stocked supermarkets.

2 garlic cloves, finely chopped

$\frac{1}{4}$ teaspoon salt

$\frac{3}{4}$ cup tahini or sesame seed paste

1 tablespoon white wine vinegar

3 tablespoons lemon juice

$\frac{1}{2}$ cup water

$\frac{1}{2}$ teaspoon ground cumin

$\frac{1}{2}$ cup chopped parsley

$\frac{1}{2}$ head of lettuce, finely chopped

Place all the ingredients in a medium-sized mixing bowl. Stir vigorously until the ingredients are blended and the consistency of the mixture is even.

Semolina Cake

MAKES 1 CAKE

This cake has a delicate sweet flavor. It will keep for weeks if refrigerated. Fine semolina can be purchased at Middle Eastern supermarkets.

$\frac{1}{2}$ cup unsalted margarine, softened

$2\frac{3}{4}$ cups sugar

1 teaspoon pure vanilla extract

2 eggs

2 cups fine semolina

1 teaspoon baking powder

$\frac{1}{2}$ teaspoon baking soda

$1\frac{1}{2}$ cups water

2 tablespoons lemon juice

Preheat the oven to 350°F. Grease a 9×12 inch baking pan.

◆ Combine the margarine, $\frac{3}{4}$ cup of the sugar, vanilla extract and eggs in a bowl. Blend with a fork until the mixture is light and creamy.

◆ Fold the semolina, baking powder and baking soda into the egg mixture. Mix well. Spread the batter in the baking pan. Bake for 35 minutes. Remove the pan from the oven and cool on a rack.

◆ While the cake cools, combine the remaining sugar with water and the lemon juice in a small saucepan. Slowly melt the sugar over a medium heat and bring the mixture to a boil. Cook for 10 minutes. Remove the saucepan from the heat and let the syrup cool until it is warm. Spoon the syrup over the top of the cake. Cut the cake into small squares and serve.

Iranian Jewish Dinner

Iranian cooking is a cuisine of savory and contrasting flavors. The centerpiece is Iran's most popular dish, rice with fruit.

Mixed Herb Platter

Kukuye

Yoghurt with Cucumbers

Rice with Fruit

Lentil Dumplings

Peach Pickles

Persian Lamb Stew

Quince Sherbet

Rice Flour Dessert

◆

Mixed Herb Platter

SERVES 6

This delightful dish of fresh herbs and feta cheese is the traditional Iranian way to begin a meal. Serve the herbs with pita bread.

1 medium-sized bunch flat-leaved parsley

1 small bunch mint sprigs

1 small bunch scallions

3 ounces fresh chives

1 small bunch fresh tarragon

1 small bunch coriander leaves

1 small bunch watercress

2 small heads of chicory

$\frac{1}{2}$ pound feta cheese, broken into small pieces

Arrange the herbs and cheese on a large platter, preferably silver or pewter.

Kukuye

SERVES 6

The Iranians are very fond of Kukuye, their own special version of omelette. This version uses zucchini.

12 eggs

1 large onion, finely chopped

8 zucchini, thinly sliced

$1\frac{1}{2}$ teaspoons ground turmeric

$\frac{1}{2}$ teaspoon salt

$\frac{1}{2}$ teaspoon black pepper

1 teaspoon sugar

$\frac{1}{4}$ cup clarified butter

Beat the eggs in a mixing bowl. Add the onion, courgettes, turmeric, salt, pepper and sugar. Mix well.

♦ In a large skillet, heat the clarified butter over a low heat until it is very hot. Add the egg mixture, cover, and cook for 5 to 7 minutes. If the omelette is entirely solid, remove it from the skillet and serve. If the omelette is still semi-solid, replace the lid and cook for a further 2 minutes.

Yoghurt with Cucumbers

SERVES 6

Yoghurt is usually served sweet with added sugar, fruit or preserves in the West. In Iran, yoghurt is used mainly in savory dishes. Serve this dish along with the Mixed Herb Platter and pita bread.

3 cups unflavored yoghurt

2 large cucumbers, peeled, thickly sliced and then quartered

2 large onions, finely chopped

$\frac{1}{2}$ cup walnuts, chopped

$\frac{1}{2}$ teaspoon salt

$\frac{1}{2}$ teaspoon white pepper

2 tablespoons chopped fresh mint

Combine all the ingredients in a large mixing bowl, and mix thoroughly, taking care not to bruise the cucumber slices.

Rice with Fruit

SERVES 6

Rice is the principal staple food of Iran. This is Iran's most celebrated rice dish.

$\frac{1}{4}$ cup clarified butter

1 onion, finely chopped

1 pound flounder fillets, cut into small pieces

$\frac{1}{2}$ teaspoon ground cinnamon

$1\frac{1}{2}$ cups fresh or canned sour cherries, pitted

$\frac{1}{2}$ cup unsalted almonds, chopped

$\frac{1}{2}$ cup currants, or raisins

$\frac{1}{2}$ cup dried apricots

$1\frac{1}{2}$ teaspoons salt

$\frac{1}{2}$ teaspoon black pepper

$2\frac{1}{2}$ cups long grain rice, rinsed and drained

5 cups water

Heat the butter in a large skillet. Add the onion and flounder pieces and sauté over a low heat for 10 minutes. Stir constantly.

♦ Add the cinnamon, cherries, almonds, currants, apricots, salt and pepper to the skillet. Stir and simmer for 3 to 4 minutes.

♦ Add the rice and water. Stir gently but well. Cover tightly and simmer over a very low heat for 55 minutes.

Lentil Dumplings

SERVES 6

Dough and lentil combinations are a protein staple of the Middle East with no real equivalent in Western cuisine. These vegetarian dumplings are filling and highly nutritious.

$1\frac{1}{2}$ cups dried brown lentils

3 cups cold water

1 cup lukewarm water

1 tablespoon grenadine syrup

1 packet active dry yeast

$3\frac{1}{2}$ cups flour

$1\frac{1}{2}$ teaspoons salt

$\frac{1}{2}$ teaspoon ground cardamom

$\frac{3}{4}$ cup clarified butter

2 large onions, finely chopped

$2\frac{1}{2}$ tablespoons brown sugar

4 cups vegetable oil

Place the lentils in a large pot and add 3 cups of cold water. Cover the pot and bring the liquid to a boil over a medium heat. Cook the lentils until the water has been absorbed and the lentils are tender, about 1 hour 15 minutes.

♦ While the lentils are cooking, make the dough. Pour the lukewarm water into a bowl and stir in the grenadine syrup. Add the yeast and stir until it dissolves. Let the mixture stand for 5 minutes.

♦ In a large bowl, combine the flour, 1 teaspoon of salt and cardamom. Add the yeast mixture and $\frac{1}{4}$ cup of the clarified butter to the flour. Stir to form a soft dough.

♦ Turn the dough out on to a lightly floured surface and knead it with a rolling pin for 10 to 12 minutes. Shape the dough into a ball, put it into a bowl, and leave it to stand in a warm place for 50 minutes.

♦ Punch down the dough and cut it in half with a sharp knife. Roll each half out into a large, flat circle. Cut the dough into 3 inch rounds with a cookie cutter.

♦ When the lentils are done, mash them with a fork to make a smooth paste. Heat the remaining clarified butter in a skillet and add the onions and lentil paste. Stir in $\frac{1}{2}$ teaspoon of salt and the brown sugar. Cook over a low heat for 5 minutes.

♦ Place a spoonful of the lentil filling into the center of each dough round. Moisten the edges of the round with water and fold the dumpling over. Press the edges together with the blunt edge of a spoon or knife to seal.

♦ Heat the vegetable oil in a large saucepan over a medium heat until it is very hot. Add the dumplings in batches of 8 and cook each batch for 3 to 5 minutes, or until the dumplings are golden brown. Remove the dumplings with a slotted spoon and drain on paper towels. Serve warm.

Peach Pickles

SERVES 6

This delightful Iranian savory should be made a week in advance. Tamarind paste is available in Middle Eastern supermarkets.

2 cups white wine vinegar

$1\frac{1}{2}$ tablespoons grated fresh ginger

$3\frac{1}{2}$ teaspoons ground coriander

4 garlic cloves, finely chopped

2 teaspoons tamarind paste

1 cup sugar

$\frac{1}{2}$ teaspoon cayenne pepper

$\frac{1}{2}$ teaspoon salt

$\frac{1}{4}$ teaspoon black pepper

$1\frac{1}{2}$ pounds fresh peaches, peeled, pitted and sliced

Place all the ingredients except the peaches in a large mixing bowl, and stir with a fork until well mixed.

♦ Put the peaches in a large pot. Add the vinegar mixture and bring to a boil over a high heat. Cook for 8 minutes. Pour the peaches and pickling liquid into a large sterilized jar. Leave it to cool. Seal the jar and refrigerate for 1 week before using.

Persian Lamb Stew

SERVES 6—8

Lots of fresh parsley is crucial to this dish. Use the flat-leaved kind for maximum flavor.

6 tablespoons butter

12 scallions, finely chopped

3 cups finely chopped parsley

$3\frac{1}{2}$ pounds lean lamb, cubed

2 quarts water

$\frac{1}{3}$ cup fresh lemon juice

1 lemon, cut into small wedges

4 cups cooked red kidney beans

1 scant tablespoon salt

2 teaspoons freshly ground black pepper

Melt 3 tablespoons of the butter in a medium stockpot. Add the scallions and parsley and sauté until the parsley turns a dark green.

♦ Melt the remaining butter in a large skillet. Add the cubed lamb and sauté until the cubes are lightly browned.

♦ Add the lamb to the stockpot. Add the water, lemon juice and lemon wedges. Stir well, cover and simmer for 1 hour 15 minutes. Stir in the kidney beans, salt and pepper. Cover and simmer for another 20 minutes, or until the lamb is tender. Serve with rice.

Quince Sherbet

SERVES 6

This distinctive Middle Eastern sherbet can be served with dairy or meat meals. Serve it in tulip or dessert glasses.

3 large ripe quinces, peeled, cored and cut into small pieces

3 cups water

3 cups sugar

$\frac{1}{4}$ cup lemon juice

Put the fruit and water into a large saucepan. Bring the mixture to a boil over a high heat. Reduce the heat to low and simmer for 40 minutes.

♦ Strain the mixture through a sieve into another saucepan. Discard any solids that remain in the sieve. Add the sugar and lemon juice and bring the mixture to a boil over a high heat. Boil for 10 minutes, stirring frequently to dissolve the sugar. Remove the saucepan from the heat and let the mixture cool for 5 minutes.

♦ Pour the sherbet mixture into a large bowl and put it in the ice compartment of the refrigerator or the freezer for 2 hours. Stir the mixture every 10 to 15 minutes to break up the ice crystals and make a smooth texture.

Rice Flour Dessert

SERVES 6 — 8

The unusual flavour of this dessert comes in part from the rose water. Well-stocked chemists sell rose water. Rice flour can either be bought or made at home by pulverizing rice in a blender or food processor.

3 tablespoons sesame oil

3 tablespoons vegetable oil

1 cup rice flour

1 quart milk

2 tablespoons rose water

1 tablespoon almond extract

$\frac{1}{2}$ cup sugar

1 teaspoon ground cardamom

$\frac{1}{8}$ teaspoon ground cinnamon

$\frac{1}{2}$ cup superfine sugar

1 cup pistachio nuts, chopped

Heat the sesame and vegetable oils together in a saucepan over a moderate heat. Stir in the rice flour and cook until the flour is a light golden brown colour. Reduce the heat to low and stir in the milk. Continue stirring until the milk and flour mixture is smooth. Add the rose water, almond extract, sugar, cardamom and cinnamon. Cook the mixture over a low heat, stirring constantly, until it thickens. Add the superfine sugar and stir until it dissolves.

♦ Pour the mixture into a lightly greased long shallow pan, sprinkle the top with the pistachio nuts, and allow it to cool and become firm. Cut into rectangles or squares.

Yemenite Jewish Supper

This unusual menu includes a broad sample of Yemenite cuisine. Some of the recipes, such as the Yemenite Herring and the Banana Cakes, originated with the Yemenite Jews. The others are enjoyed by Jews and Muslims alike. As meat in Yemen is neither cheap or plentiful, the cuisine makes great use of every part of the animal.

Flatbread
Hilbeh
Zhug
Liver and Kidney Stew
Herring Yemen-Style
Banana Cakes

♦

Flatbread

MAKES 8—10 BREADS

This very simple bread has a lot of flavor. Serve it warm with Hilbeh and Zhug at the beginning of the meal.

3 cups wholewheat flour

1 teaspoon salt

1 cup warm water

$\frac{1}{4}$ cup vegetable oil

In a large mixing bowl, combine the flour, salt and water. Stir until the consistency of the dough is soft and even throughout. Turn the dough out on to a lightly floured surface and knead for 10 to 12 minutes. Form the dough into a ball. Place the ball in a mixing bowl and cover with plastic wrap. Leave it to stand for $2\frac{1}{2}$ hours.

♦ Divide the dough into balls with a diameter of about $1\frac{1}{2}$ inches. Roll the balls into small thin circles. Let the dough rounds stand for 25 minutes.

♦ In a large, heavy skillet heat the oil until it is very hot. Place the dough circles one at a time in the hot oil and cook for 2 minutes each over a moderate heat. Turn the the circles over and sauté for 1 minute longer.

♦ After each bread circle is cooked, place it in a dish lined with paper towels to drain. Keep warm.

Hilbeh

SERVES 6—8

Hilbeh is a dip traditionally eaten with flatbread at the start of a meal. Fenugreek seeds are available in Middle Eastern supermarkets.

3 teaspoons fenugreek seeds

1 cup cold water

3 garlic cloves, finely chopped

1 cup fresh coriander leaves, very finely chopped

$\frac{1}{4}$ teaspoon salt

$1\frac{1}{2}$ tablespoons lemon juice

$\frac{1}{4}$ teaspoon cayenne pepper

Put the fenugreek seeds into a small bowl and add the cold water. Soak the seeds for 12 hours. Drain well.

♦ In a large wooden mixing bowl, combine the fenugreek seeds with the garlic, coriander, salt, lemon juice and cayenne pepper. Combine thoroughly until the mixture is a smooth paste. Place the mixture in a glass bowl, cover and chill before serving.

Zhug

SERVES 6—8

Zhug is a spicy dip with a markedly different taste from Hilbeh. Serve it chilled.

3 cardamom pods

1 teaspoon black peppercorns

2 teaspoons caraway seeds

4 hot chili peppers, finely chopped

1 cup coriander leaves, finely chopped

1 cup watercress, finely chopped

6 garlic cloves, finely chopped

$\frac{1}{2}$ teaspoon salt

$\frac{1}{4}$ cup cold water

Grind the cardamom pods, peppercorns and caraway seeds into a powder using a mortar and pestle. Combine the spice powder with the chilis, coriander, watercress, garlic, salt and water in a bowl. Mix well.

♦ Place the mixture in a small saucepan and bring it to a boil over a moderate heat. Reduce the heat to low and simmer for 10 minutes. Spoon the mixture into a glass jar, cover, and chill.

Liver and Kidney Stew

SERVES 6—8

This delicious stew will tempt even confirmed liver-haters. It is important to follow the soaking directions in order for the liver to be kosher.

2 pounds fresh lamb liver

4 lamb kidneys, skin and core removed

$\frac{1}{4}$ cup vegetable oil

2 large onions, coarsely chopped

5 garlic cloves, finely chopped

1 teaspoon ground turmeric

$1\frac{1}{2}$ cups tomato paste

$1\frac{1}{2}$ teaspoons ground coriander

$\frac{3}{4}$ teaspoon ground cumin

2 cardamom pods

$\frac{1}{2}$ cup water

1 tablespoon coarsely chopped fresh coriander

1 tablespoon coarsely chopped parsley

1 teaspoon salt

$\frac{1}{2}$ teaspoon black pepper

Soak the liver and kidneys in lightly salted cold water for 40 minutes. Drain the meat well and pat dry with paper towels. Cut the liver into small cubes, removing any tough membranes and tubes. Cut the kidneys into cubes.

♦ Heat the oil in a large, heavy skillet. Add the onion, garlic and turmeric and sauté over a low heat for 5 minutes. Add the liver and kidney cubes and sauté for a further 10 minutes, or until the meat is lightly browned all over.

♦ Add the tomato paste, dried coriander, cumin, cardamom pods, water, fresh coriander, parsley, salt and pepper. Cover and simmer over a low heat for 90 minutes. Check every half hour adding water if necessary. Serve hot.

Herring Yemen-style

SERVES 6—8

Herring Yemen-style was originally prepared over an open fire. This recipe has been adapted for use in modern kitchens.

4 salt herrings, cut into small pieces

4 tablespoons coriander leaves chopped

1 tablespoon fresh or 1 teaspoon dried marjoram

$\frac{1}{4}$ teaspoon salt

$\frac{1}{4}$ teaspoon black pepper

1 large pimento, finely chopped

1 tablespoon chopped parsley

1 cup finely chopped onion

Place the herring pieces in a large glass or ceramic, not metal, baking dish. Cover the herring with the coriander, marjoram, salt, pepper, pimento, parsley and onion. Cover the dish and marinate in the refrigerator for 6 hours.

♦ Preheat the oven to broil. Remove the herring pieces from the marinade and place them in an ovenproof dish. Broil until they are lightly browned, about 15 minutes.

Banana Cakes

SERVES 6—8

The perfect ending to a Middle Eastern meal, these banana cakes have a sweet, nutty flavor.

4 cups flour

3 teaspoons sugar

$1\frac{1}{2}$ teaspoons salt

4 tablespoons margarine

4 bananas, mashed to a paste

$\frac{1}{2}$-1 cup water

$\frac{3}{4}$ cup vegetable oil

Combine the flour, sugar, salt, margarine and mashed bananas in a large mixing bowl. Mix well. Add enough of the water to stiffen the dough. Cover the bowl and leave it to stand for 25 minutes.

♦ Turn the dough out on to a lightly floured surface. Roll the dough out into a thin sheet. Cut the dough into 4 inch squares.

♦ In a large, heavy skillet, heat the oil until it is very hot. Sauté the dough squares, one at a time until they are golden brown, about 3 minutes for the first side and 2 minutes for the second. Serve warm.

Syrian Lebanese Dinner

Modern Israeli cooking is strongly influenced by the cuisine of the Jews of Lebanon and Syria. Felafel, for example, which is assumed by many to be an Israeli invention, is in fact an age-old creation of the Syrian-Lebanese Jews.

Chard Soup with Lentils
Stuffed Artichokes
Felafel
Lebanese Cauliflower
Potato Salad
Nut Pudding

♦

Chard Soup with Lentils

SERVES 6—8

Yet another version of Middle Eastern lentil soup. Kale or fresh spinach may be substituted for the chard.

2 cups dried brown lentils

8 cups water

$\frac{1}{4}$ cup olive oil

2 large onions, finely chopped

6 garlic cloves, coarsely chopped

2 cups torn Swiss chard leaves, tough stems removed

$\frac{1}{4}$ cup chopped coriander

$\frac{1}{2}$ teaspoon salt

$\frac{1}{4}$ teaspoon black pepper

$\frac{1}{4}$ cup lemon juice

Pick over the lentils and wash them. Put the lentils into a large saucepan and add the water. Cover and cook over a medium heat for 1 hour.

♦ When the lentils have cooked for 50 minutes, heat the olive oil in a skillet over a low heat. Add the onions, garlic and chard and sauté for 8 minutes, stirring constantly.

♦ Add the chard mixture to the lentils. Add the coriander, salt, pepper and lemon juice and stir well. Cover the saucepan and simmer over a low heat for 20 minutes. Serve hot.

Stuffed Artichokes

SERVES 8

Lamb is the principal meat served in Lebanon and Syria.

1 tablespoon olive oil

1 onion, finely chopped

$\frac{1}{4}$ cup pine nuts

1 pound ground lamb

2 tablespoons chopped parsley

$\frac{1}{2}$ teaspoon black pepper

$\frac{1}{4}$ teaspoon salt

8 large artichokes, stems trimmed and outermost leaves removed

4 cups water

2 tablespoons margarine

$\frac{1}{4}$ cup lemon juice

Heat the oil in a small saucepan. Add the onion and pine nuts and cook for 3 to 5 minutes over a low heat.

♦ Combine the ground lamb with the onions and pine nuts in a small mixing bowl. Add the parsley, pepper and salt. Mix thoroughly.

♦ Stuff the artichokes with the meat mixture, inserting small quantities between the leaves with a teaspoon.

♦ Place the artichokes upright in 2 large saucepans, 4 in each pot. Fill each pot with 2 cups water. Reduce the heat to low and cover the pots. Steam the artichokes for 45 minutes and then drain well.

♦ In a small saucepan, melt the margarine and add in the lemon juice. Pour the mixture over the artichokes and simmer for 15 minutes. Serve warm.

Felafel

SERVES 8

If you are serving felafel with a meat meal, be sure to use only tahini sauce and not a yoghurt-tahini mix.

1 cup dried fava beans

1 cup dried chick peas

3 garlic cloves, chopped

1 medium onion, finely chopped

$\frac{1}{2}$ cup finely chopped parsley

$\frac{1}{4}$ teaspoon cayenne pepper

1 teaspoon ground coriander

$\frac{1}{2}$ teaspoon ground cumin

1 teaspoon baking soda

$\frac{1}{2}$ teaspoon salt

$\frac{1}{4}$ teaspoon black pepper

4 cups vegetable oil

8 pita breads

1 cup shredded lettuce

1 cup ripe tomatoes, cubed

$\frac{1}{2}$ cup tahini sauce

Soak the fava beans in 2 cups cold water for 48 hours.

♦ Soak the chickpeas in 2 cups cold water for 12 hours.

♦ Drain the fava beans well. Drain the chickpeas well and rub them through a sieve.

♦ Combine the fava beans and sieved chickpeas with the garlic and onion in a large wooden mixing bowl. Chop together until the consistency is even.

♦ Mix in the parsley, cayenne pepper, coriander, cumin, baking soda, salt and pepper. Combine thoroughly and stand for 20 minutes.

♦ Shape the mixture into about 30 balls and leave for 30 minutes.

♦ In a medium-sized saucepan heat the oil until it is very hot. Drop in as many felafel balls as will fill the saucepan without crowding. Cook the balls for 6 or 7 minutes. Drain on paper towels. Repeat the process with the remaining felafel balls.

♦ Slice the top off each pita bread and open it up. Place 3 to 4 felafel balls in each pocket with some lettuce and tomato. Top with tahini sauce.

Lebanese Cauliflower

SERVES 6 — 8

The addition of tahini sauce gives this cauliflower dish an exotic flavor.

1 large cauliflower, trimmed

1 cup tahini sauce

2 tablespoons sesame seeds

$\frac{1}{2}$ teaspoon lemon juice

$\frac{1}{2}$ teaspoon paprika

$\frac{1}{2}$ small onion, finely chopped

Place the cauliflower in a medium-sized saucepan and add 4 cups cold water. Cover the pan and steam the cauliflower for 12 to 14 minutes, or until tender.

♦ Combine the tahini, sesame seeds, lemon juice, paprika and onion. Stir well.

♦ Drain the cauliflower and place it on a serving dish and pour the tahini sauce mixture over it while the cauliflower is still hot. Serve hot.

Potato Salad

SERVES 6 — 8

Mint and lots of parsley give this potato salad a refreshingly different taste.

8 potatoes, unpeeled
1 small onion, finely chopped
$\frac{1}{2}$ cup finely chopped parsley
1 teaspoon dried mint or 1 tablespoon chopped fresh mint
$\frac{1}{4}$ teaspoon black pepper
2 garlic cloves, very finely chopped
$\frac{1}{2}$ cup lemon juice
$\frac{1}{2}$ cup olive oil

Cook the potatoes in a large pan of boiling salted water for 10 to 15 minutes, or until they are tender but not mushy.
♦ Drain the potatoes and cut them into chunks. Put the chunks into a large salad bowl.
♦ In a large mixing bowl, combine the onions, parsley, mint, pepper, garlic, lemon juice and olive oil. Mix well. Pour the dressing over the potatoes. Toss well. Serve at room temperature.

Nut Pudding

SERVES 8

This traditional Syrian nut pudding is enjoyed by both Jews and Muslims. Use white, not green, pistachio nuts.

$4\frac{1}{2}$ cups light cream or non-dairy cream substitute
$\frac{1}{2}$ cup ground rice
$\frac{1}{4}$ teaspoon salt
$\frac{1}{2}$ cup sugar
$\frac{1}{2}$ cup ground unsalted almonds
$\frac{1}{2}$ cup ground unsalted pistachio nuts
2 tablespoons grenadine syrup

In a medium-sized saucepan, bring the cream to a boil. Add the ground rice, salt and sugar. Simmer over a medium heat for 5 minutes, stirring constantly.
♦ Stir in the ground almonds, ground pistachios and grenadine syrup. Reduce the heat to low and simmer for 2 minutes, stirring constantly.
♦ Remove the saucepan from the heat and let the mixture cool until it is warm. Spoon the pudding into small individual dessert dishes and chill. Serve cold.

Israeli
Middle Eastern Lunch

The Israelis are noted for their abundant breakfasts and lunches, which, perhaps as a result of the warm climate, feature fresh fruits and vegetables and salads. This menu consists of Middle Eastern specialties in that tradition. Pita bread is eaten throughout the area at every meal. The tarama salad is really Greek in origin, but is commonly served in Israel. Dessert, if there needed to be one, would be fresh fruit. With the possible exception of the spiced fish, any of these dishes could be served for breakfast as well.

Hummus
Spiced Fish
Pita Bread
Tabouleh
Lentil and Feta Cheese Salad
Tarama Salad

♦

Hummus

SERVES 6—8

This garlicky chickpea dip is a favorite appetizer in the Middle East. Serve it with pita bread or crudités.

4 cups of cooked chickpeas, drained

$\frac{1}{2}$ cup tahini (sesame seed paste)

1 medium-sized onion, quartered

$\frac{1}{2}$ cup fresh lemon juice

2 garlic cloves, chopped

$\frac{1}{2}$ teaspoon paprika

$\frac{1}{2}$ teaspoon dried coriander

$\frac{1}{2}$ teaspoon ground cumin

$\frac{1}{2}$ teaspoon salt

$\frac{1}{2}$ teaspoon freshly ground black pepper

$1\frac{1}{2}$ tablespoons water

3 tablespoons fresh parsley, coarsely chopped

Put the chickpeas, tahini, onion, lemon juice, garlic, paprika, coriander, cumin, salt, pepper and water into a food processor or electric blender. Blend until smooth and creamy. Pour the hummus into a serving dish. Garnish with the chopped parsley.

Spiced Fish

SERVES 6

This simple but flavorful way to prepare fish makes an excellent entrée for dairy menus.

$\frac{1}{4}$ cup lemon juice

$\frac{1}{2}$ teaspoon ground ginger

$\frac{1}{2}$ teaspoon finely chopped garlic

$\frac{1}{4}$ teaspoon ground cumin

$\frac{1}{2}$ teaspoon paprika

$\frac{1}{4}$ teaspoon cayenne pepper

$\frac{1}{4}$ teaspoon ground turmeric

$\frac{1}{2}$ teaspoon salt

1 cup white wine

3 pounds flounder fillets

Preheat the oven to 375°F. In a small mixing bowl, combine all the ingredients except the flounder fillets. Mix well.

♦ Arrange the fillets in a large baking dish and pour the sauce over them. Bake for 15 minutes. Serve hot.

Pita Bread

MAKES 20 SMALL BREADS

Small round flat breads of pita are increasingly popular in the West. When cut in half, the breads form convenient pockets for sandwiches.

2 envelopes dry yeast
1 teaspoon sugar
$1\frac{1}{4}$ cups warm water
4 cups flour
1 teaspoon salt

Preheat the oven to 475°F.

♦ Put the yeast and sugar in a mixing bowl, add the warm water and stir lightly to dissolve the dry ingredients. Stir in the flour and salt and continue stirring until a dough forms. Knead the dough for 8 to 10 minutes. Divide the dough into 20 balls. Roll out each dough ball to $\frac{3}{8}$ inch thickness. Cover the rolled out circles with a damp cloth and leave to rise for 30 minutes. Roll out the circles again and leave to rise for another 30 minutes.

♦ Put the 20 dough circles on a well-greased baking sheet. Bake the pita for 3 minutes or until the breads are puffed up and lightly browned. Serve at once or store in a plastic bag to keep moist.

Tabouleh

SERVES 6

Serve tabouleh as an appetizer with pita bread. Be sure to use fresh, not dried, mint.

1 cup bulgur wheat
2 cups boiling water
$\frac{1}{2}$ cup chopped scallion
5 tablespoons chopped fresh mint
2 medium-sized tomatoes, seeded and chopped
1 cup chopped fresh parsley
5 tablespoons olive oil
6 tablespoons fresh lemon juice
$\frac{1}{2}$ teaspoon salt
$\frac{1}{2}$ teaspoon freshly ground black pepper
10 large lettuce leaves

Put the bulgur into a bowl and add the boiling water. Stir, cover the bowl, and leave to stand for 35 minutes.

♦ Drain the bulgur, squeezing out any remaining water between the palms of your hands. Put the bulgur into a serving bowl. Add the scallions, mint, tomatoes and parsley. Toss gently. Add the olive oil. Stir until well mixed. Add the lemon juice, salt and pepper. Stir until well mixed.

♦ Serve the tabouleh in the serving bowl or on individual plates. Use the lettuce leaves as scoops to eat the tabouleh.

Lentil and Feta Cheese Salad

SERVES 6

This hearty salad is a meal in itself. Serve it with pita bread.

$1\frac{1}{2}$ cups brown lentils

1 bay leaf

$\frac{1}{2}$ teaspoon dried basil

2 garlic cloves, crushed

$\frac{1}{2}$ cup diced celery

1 small onion, chopped

$\frac{3}{4}$ cup crumbled feta cheese

$\frac{1}{2}$ cup chopped fresh chives

For the dressing:

6 tablespoons olive oil

3 tablespoons wine vinegar

$\frac{1}{8}$ teaspoon dried oregano

$\frac{1}{2}$ teaspoon salt

$\frac{1}{2}$ teaspoon freshly ground black pepper

Soak the lentils in 3 cups cold water for 2 hours. Drain.
◆ Put the lentils into a saucepan and add enough cold water to cover them completely. Add the bay leaf, basil and one of the garlic cloves. Bring to a boil and then reduce the heat. Simmer, covered, for 20 minutes.
◆ Add the celery and onion. Add enough additional water to cover the lentils. Cover the saucepan and simmer for 10 more minutes.
◆ Drain the lentils. Discard the bay leaf and garlic clove.
◆ Put the lentils into a serving bowl. Add the feta cheese and chives. Toss.
◆ Put the olive oil, vinegar, oregano, remaining garlic clove, salt and pepper into a jar with a tightly fitting lid. Cover tightly and shake until well blended.
◆ Pour the dressing over the lentil salad and toss. Let the salad stand at room temperature for 2 hours, tossing occasionally, before serving.

Tarama Salad

SERVES 6—8

This dip makes a good appetizer for lunch. Serve it with sliced cucumbers and tomatoes and pita bread.

3 large potatoes

3 tablespoons milk

4 ounces red caviar or red roe

6 tablespoons water

$\frac{1}{4}$ cup lemon juice

1 small onion, finely chopped

$\frac{3}{4}$ cup olive oil

Peel the potatoes. Cook them in boiling water until very soft, about 20 minutes.
◆ Drain the potatoes and put them into a mixing bowl. By hand or with an electric beater, mash the potatoes, slowly adding the milk, until smooth. Add the caviar and water to the potatoes. Mix well. Add the lemon juice and onion to the mixture and mix briefly. Slowly beat in the olive oil. Continue to beat until a smooth paste is formed.

Mixed Herb Platter ABOVE, *a traditional Iranian Jewish first course, is served here with Yoghurt and Cucumbers (page 34).*

♦

Rice with Fruit BELOW *is Iran's most celebrated rice dish (page 35).*

Zhug ABOVE *is a spicy dip from the
Yemen (page 41).*

♦

Banana Cakes BELOW LEFT *make a perfect ending
to a Middle Eastern meal (page 42).*

♦

Felafel BELOW RIGHT *is a traditional Middle Eastern
dish, served in Pita Bread (page 45).*

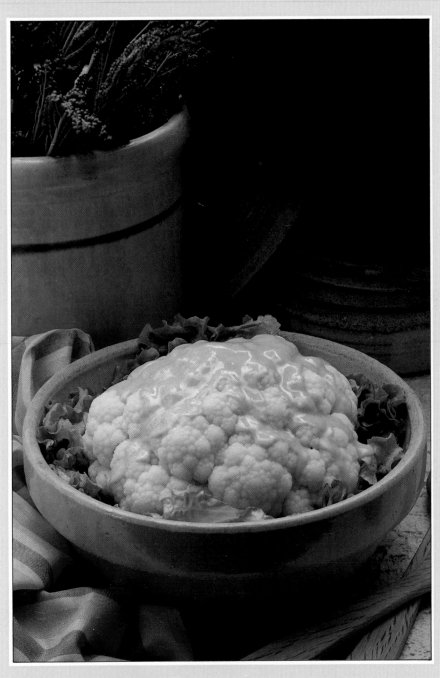

Lebanese Cauliflower topped with Tahini Sauce makes an exotic vegetable side dish (page 45).

Russia

and Eastern Europe

The Khazar Jewish kingdom was a fascinating episode in Russian Jewish History. The Khazars were a pagan, nomadic tribe living in the area between the Black Sea and the Caspian Sea and to the north. Their king converted to Judaism in about 700. In the three centuries that followed, many Khazars became Jews and Jews from elsewhere were invited to settle in the kingdom. The Russians to the north began attacking the kingdom in 970, and in 1016 a combined Russian-Byzantine attack destroyed the kingdom. The Jews dispersed into Russia, Armenia, Byzantium and the Mediterranean coast. It is likely that many of the Jews of these regions are descended from Khazar refugees.

Jews have lived in Russia and the Eastern European countries ever since. In the eleventh and twelfth centuries and again in the fifteenth century many Russians converted to Judaism. The Jews were always under suspicion, however, and in 1804 the Pale of Settlement was established. This forced Jews in Russia, the Ukraine and Poland to live in ghettos and restricted areas. Their economic and educational opportunities were extremely limited. Despite this and despite continuing persecution, the Jews of Eastern Europe developed vital and thriving communities. Even so, millions fled oppression for new lives in America, England and elsewhere. More recently, many Soviet Jews have emigrated to Israel and America.

Because so many of these Jews left their homelands for Western Europe and America, it is their cooking that is often identified as 'Jewish'. Traditional dishes such as cholent, kugel, kasha, blintzes and stuffed cabbage are all part of this cuisine. The Jews of Poland were famous for their herring dishes and developed arguably the definitive version of stuffed cabbage. They also created a huge variety of kugels (baked puddings). The Romanian Jews shared their Gentile counterparts' enjoyment of dishes with a sour flavor. The Romanians were also fine bakers, rivaling the famed pastry empire of Vienna. Hungarian Jews were fond of fruit soups. They also developed their own distinct version of lesco, a traditional Hungarian vegetable dish. All Hungarian cooking, both Jewish and Gentile, relies heavily on exotic seasonings such as nutmeg and paprika. Kohlrabi, a vegetable unusual in Western-style cooking, was also popular. The Jews of Yugoslavia enjoyed vegetable caviar, lamb and the famous dessert preserves called slatko.

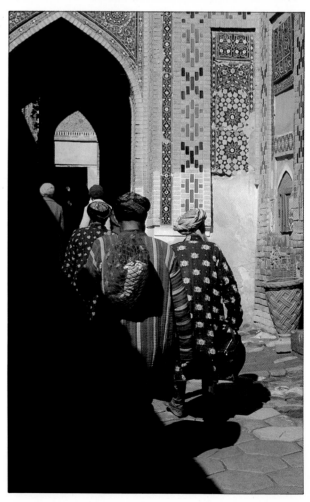

Jews settled all over Russia and Eastern Europe, from Leningrad to Samarkand and Bucharest. Their diverse cultural history is reflected in their cuisine.

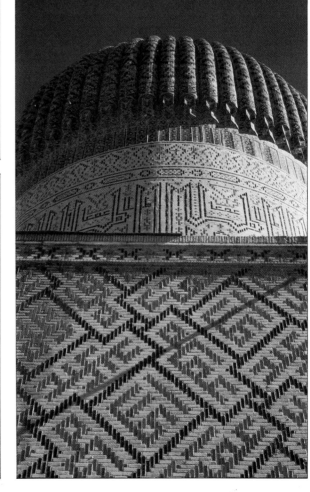

Russian Sabbath Dinner

This traditional dinner might have been served on Friday or Saturday night in a relatively prosperous Jewish household in Moscow at the turn of the century. It shows traditional Jewish and Russian influences, as well as the influence of the French. It should be noted that sturgeon caviar, which was often eaten by the more cosmopolitan Jews of Moscow and St Petersburg, was not eaten by the more orthodox Jews, who felt that, as a bottom feeder, the sturgeon was unclean. However, as sturgeon caviar is not unkosher in the strict sense of the word, it is included as an authentic part of the meal. Three different liquors were served with the meal, in addition to the traditional red grape wine used for the blessing. A white wine or aperitif was served before the meal or with the appetizer, red wine was served with the main course, and flavored vodka or slivovitz, a potent fruit brandy, was served with dessert.

Chopped Chicken Livers

New Potatoes with Caviar

Pickled Herring in

Raspberry Vinegar

Stuffed Peppers

Russian Egg Drop Soup

Cholent

Cabbage Salad

Russian Seedcake

Zakuski: Chopped Chicken Livers

SERVES 6—10

A traditional Friday night dinner in a comfortable Russian-Jewish home would start with a zakuski, a variety of different appetizers served together. A typical zakuski would consist of four to ten separate dishes. Each person would be served with a little of each zakuski on a traditional enamelled plate.

1 pound fresh chicken livers
$\frac{1}{4}$ cup mayonnaise
2 hard-boiled eggs
$\frac{1}{4}$ cup chopped celery
$\frac{1}{4}$ cup chopped onion
$\frac{1}{2}$ teaspoon salt
$\frac{1}{2}$ teaspoon freshly ground black pepper

Put the chicken livers into a saucepan and cover completely with cold water. Bring to a boil and cook for 10 to 12 minutes. Drain the livers well.

♦ In a large mixing bowl, combine the livers with the mayonnaise and eggs. Mash the mixture with a fork. Add the celery, onion, salt and pepper. Mash until the mixture has an even, fine consistency.

♦ Put the mixture into a serving bowl, cover, and chill for at least 1 hour before serving. Serve with crusty bread, melba toast or crackers.

Zakuski: New Potatoes with Caviar

SERVES 6—8

6 medium-sized new potatoes
1 ounce black caviar
1 ounce red caviar
8 hard-boiled egg yolks, crumbled
3 lemons, quartered

Cook the potatoes in a large pot of boiling water until they are tender, about 20 to 30 minutes. Drain well.

♦ When the potatoes are cool enough to handle, cut them in half lengthwise. Scoop a small pocket out of each half with a teaspoon.

♦ Fill six of the potato halves with the black caviar; fill the remaining halves with the red caviar. Sprinkle the crumbled egg yolks over each potato. Put both a red and black potato half on each zakuski plate and garnish with lemon wedges.

Zakuski: Pickled Herring

SERVES 6—10

$1\frac{1}{2}$ pounds pickled herring (rollmops)

$\frac{1}{2}$ cup raspberry vinegar

$\frac{1}{2}$ cup small onions, diced

1 teaspoon freshly ground black pepper

$\frac{1}{2}$ teaspoon tarragon

$\frac{1}{2}$ cup white wine

$\frac{1}{2}$ cup cooked peas

Drain the herring well and set aside. Discard any onions or other ingredients packed with the herring.

♦ Put the raspberry vinegar, onions, pepper, tarragon and white wine in a large glass or ceramic, but not metal, bowl. Add the herring, which should be completely covered by the liquid; if not, add equal amounts of white wine and vinegar until the herring is covered. Cover and chill for at least 12 hours.

♦ Just before serving, add the peas to the herring and marinade and mix gently.

Zakuski: Stuffed Peppers

SERVES 4—8

4 large green peppers

1 pound ground beef

$\frac{1}{4}$ cup cooked rice

1 small onion, finely chopped

$\frac{1}{4}$ teaspoon salt

$\frac{1}{2}$ teaspoon black pepper

1 egg yolk

$\frac{1}{4}$ cup red wine

$\frac{1}{2}$ cup chopped mushrooms

$\frac{1}{4}$ cup seeded and chopped fresh tomatoes

$\frac{1}{4}$ cup fresh lemon juice

2 tablespoons sugar

$\frac{1}{4}$ teaspoon paprika

2 tablespoons brandy

$1\frac{1}{2}$ teaspoons raspberry or cider vinegar

Preheat the oven to 375°F. Cut the tops off the green peppers and carefully discard the seeds. Blanch the peppers in a large pot of boiling water for 3 minutes. Drain well and set aside.

♦ In a large mixing bowl combine the minced beef, rice, onion, salt, pepper, egg yolk, wine and $\frac{1}{4}$ cup of mushrooms. Mix well. Stuff the blanched peppers with the mixture.

♦ Place the peppers on their sides in a large baking dish. Add the vinegar and enough water to fill the dish to a depth of 2 inches. Cover the dish and bake for 35 minutes.

♦ When the peppers have been in the oven for 30 minutes, combine the remaining mushrooms with the tomatoes, lemon juice, sugar, paprika and brandy in a small saucepan. Cover the saucepan and simmer over a very low heat for 5 minutes. Pour the mixture over the stuffed peppers.

♦ Reduce the oven temperature to 300°F. Bake the stuffed peppers, uncovered, for a further 15 minutes. Serve warm.

Russian Egg Drop Soup

SERVES 8—10

8 cups chicken broth

3 cups chicken, cooked and shredded

$\frac{1}{4}$ cup white wine

4 cups fine egg noodles

$\frac{1}{2}$ teaspoon salt

$\frac{1}{4}$ teaspoon dill

$\frac{1}{2}$ cup finely chopped celery

2 large carrots, quartered

1 sprig parsley

4 eggs, well beaten

Pour the chicken broth into a large saucepan. Add the chicken meat, wine, egg noodles, dill, salt, celery, carrots and parsley. Bring the soup to the boil. Reduce the heat and simmer for 18 to 20 minutes over a low heat.

♦ Bring the soup back to a furious boil. Beat the eggs in with a fork. Remove the pan from the heat when the eggs become cloud-like. Serve hot.

Cholent

SERVES 8—10

Of all the recipes ever collected for this legendary Jewish dish, no two are exactly alike. All involve some variation on beans, beef and potatoes, with some versions including barley as well. Cholent was traditionally prepared on Friday afternoon and then taken to the baker's oven, where it was cooked slowly in the banked fires until Saturday afternoon, when it was removed and served as the Sabbath meal.

$\frac{1}{2}$ pound dried baby lima beans

$\frac{1}{2}$ pound dried red kidney beans

$\frac{1}{2}$ pound dried yellow split peas

$\frac{1}{2}$ pound dried lentils

4 tablespoons margarine

4 large onions, quartered

2 garlic cloves, crushed

1 teaspoon black pepper

1 teaspoon salt

2 teaspoons paprika

4 pounds beef brisket

3 cups white wine

$1\frac{1}{2}$ pounds potatoes, peeled and quartered

Preheat the oven to 450°F. Place the dried legumes in separate bowls. Add 3 cups of cold water to each bowl and leave the legumes to soak overnight. Drain well.

♦ Melt the margarine in a large heavy pot. Add the onions and brown them. Add the garlic, pepper, salt and paprika. Add the brisket and brown it.

♦ Add the wine, 4 cups cold water, all the legumes and the potatoes. Bring the liquid to a boil. Cover the pot tightly and place it in the oven. Bake for 1 hour, then reduce the heat to 300°F and bake for a further 90 minutes.

♦ Remove the brisket from the pot and let it rest for 10 minutes before slicing. Arrange the legumes and potatoes around the brisket and spoonover the broth.

Cabbage Salad

SERVES 8

This light, crisp dish is a welcome contrast to the hearty flavors of the cholent. Be sure the cabbage is fresh and the salad is served well chilled.

> 6 cups white cabbage, shredded
>
> 1 small onion, diced
>
> ¼ cup chopped scallions
>
> 2 tablespoons diced chili peppers
>
> ½ teaspoon salt
>
> 4 tablespoons chopped fresh coriander
>
> 3 tablespoons olive oil
>
> ½ cup lime juice
>
> 1 tablespoon Dijon-style mustard
>
> 1 tablespoon honey

Combine all the ingredients in a large serving bowl and toss well. Chill for 20 to 30 minutes before serving.

Russian Seedcake

MAKES 1 CAKE

This simple yet deliciously aromatic cake is the perfect ending to any meal. Serve it with Russian-style tea — stir a spoonful of preserves or rum, or both, into each glass of tea.

> 2 cups sugar
>
> 2 cups sweet butter
>
> 10 eggs
>
> 4 cups flour
>
> 1 teaspoon salt
>
> 2 teaspoons baking powder
>
> 3 teaspoons pure vanilla extract
>
> 2 tablespoons sesame seeds
>
> 2 tablespoons caraway seeds
>
> ½ cup orange juice
>
> ½ teaspoon cinnamon
>
> ½ cup raspberry or plum preserves

Preheat the oven to 350°F. Cream the sugar and butter together in a large mixing bowl. Add the eggs, two at a time, beating well after each addition.

♦ Add the flour, salt, baking powder, vanilla extract, sesame seeds, caraway seeds, orange juice and cinnamon. Beat for 7 minutes. Butter and flour a 12 inch diameter cake pan. Pour in the batter and bake for 1 hour or until a cocktail stick inserted in the center of the cake comes out clean.

♦ Remove the cake from the oven and leave it to cool to room temperature. Spread the top of the cake with raspberry or plum preserves and serve.

Russian Dairy Lunch

*This dairy lunch of traditional Russian specialities might have been
served in the cosmopolitan home of a wealthy family or as a festive meal
in a poorer household. The Russians are particularly fond of mushrooms
in any form. This menu uses both dried and pickled mushrooms. The
dessert, assuming anyone has room for it, is the famed Charlotte Russe.*

Gefilte Fish Russe
Kasha
Fish Soup
Bliny
Soured Cream
Charlotte Russe

Gefilte Fish Russe

SERVES 8—10

Gefilte fish is a staple of Jewish cooking throughout Europe, Russia and America. It is made a little differently by each group, and each group claims to have originated the dish and to have the best recipe. The dish was originally made as the stuffing for baked fish. Eventually the stuffing itself became the dish.

2 pounds fresh white fish fillets (set aside the heads, skin and bones)
2 pounds fresh carp fillets (set aside the heads, skin and bones)
2 pounds fresh pike fillets (set aside the heads, skin and bones)
2 tablespoons salt
4 large onions, finely chopped
4 eggs, beaten
½ cup matzoh meal
2 tablespoons sugar
2 carrots, cut into fine julienne strips
3 carrots, peeled and cut into 1 inch rounds

Put the reserved fish heads, skin and bones into a large stock pot. Add 8 cups of cold water, 1 teaspoon salt and 1½ teaspoons black pepper. Bring the liquid to a boil and cook, uncovered, over a high heat for 40 minutes. Strain the fish stock into another pot and discard the heads, skin and bones.

♦ Finely chop the fish fillets. Put the chopped fish into a large bowl and add the onions, eggs, matzoh meal, sugar, remaining salt and pepper, julienne carrots and 1 cup cold water. Mix well until the consistency is even. Shape the fish mixture into balls about 2 inches in diameter.

♦ Bring the strained fish stock to a boil over a low heat. Add the carrot slices. Drop the fish balls into the stock and cover the pot. Simmer over a low heat for 1 hour. Remove the cover and simmer for another 45 minutes. Remove the pot from the heat and let the gefilte fish cool in the liquid to room temperature.

♦ Remove the gefilte fish and put them into a glass or ceramic serving bowl. Strain the stock again and pour it over the fish. Add the sliced carrots from the stock. Cover the bowl and chill for 2 hours before serving. Serve with horseradish.

Kasha

SERVES 8—10

Few foods are as deceiving as kasha. In Russia, kasha can mean any cereal; outside Russia, it almost always means buckwheat groats. Kasha sounds plain, mealy and unappetizing, but is in fact savory and flavorful. Packaged, roasted buckwheat groats are available in any store, in three types: fine, medium and coarse. For true authenticity, use coarse groats. This dish can be made with just fresh mushrooms, but the rich aroma imparted by the dried mushrooms should not be missed.

½ pound dried mushrooms
2 cups kasha (coarse buckwheat groats)
2 eggs, beaten
1½ teaspoons salt
5 cups boiling water
½ pound butter
3 cups small onions, quartered
½ pound fresh mushrooms, quartered
3 tablespoons finely chopped scallions

Put the dried mushrooms into a small bowl and add enough warm water to cover. Let the mushrooms soak for 1 hour. Drain well. Trim away any tough stems and cut any large mushrooms in half.

♦ Put the kasha into a medium-sized mixing bowl. Fold the beaten eggs into the kasha.

♦ In a large, heavy skillet, sauté the kasha and egg mixture over a medium heat, until the kasha begins to become dry. Add the salt, 4 cups of the boiling water and 8 tablespoons of the butter. Cover the skillet tightly and reduce the heat to low. Simmer for 20 minutes, stirring at 5-minute intervals.

♦ Add the remaining boiling water to the skillet. Cover and simmer for a further 5 minutes. Turn the heat off. Leave it to stand for 15 minutes.

♦ Turn the heat on again and add the onions, dried mushrooms, fresh mushrooms and scallions . Stir briefly. Reduce the heat to medium and add the remaining butter. Cook, stirring constantly, until the mushrooms are cooked and the kasha is dry again, about 3 to 5 minutes.

Fish Soup

SERVES 8—10

Deliciously light and savory, this Russian fish soup is traditionally made during the summer and autumn months.

7 cups water

1½ cups finely chopped onions

2 teaspoons finely chopped fresh parsley

¼ teaspoon finely grated lemon rind

1 bay leaf

¼ teaspoon black pepper

1 pound halibut steaks, cut into pieces

1 pound swordfish steaks, cut into pieces

½ cup heavy cream

1 cup white wine

¼ teaspoon white pepper

1 garlic clove, crushed

2 large cucumbers, peeled and cut into slices

2 cups tomatoes, peeled, seeded and cut into pieces

½ cup black olives, pitted and halved

In a very large soup pot, combine the water, onions, parsley, lemon rind, bay leaf and black pepper. Bring the liquid to a boil, reduce the heat and simmer for 2 minutes.

♦ Add the fish to the pot and simmer for 5 minutes. Reduce the heat to low and simmer for a further 5 minutes.

♦ Add the cream, white wine, white pepper, garlic clove, cucumbers and tomatoes to the pot. Simmer over a low heat for 5 minutes. Do not let the soup boil.

♦ Remove the pot from the heat. Stir in the olives. Leave the soup to stand for 30 seconds. Stir again and serve.

Bliny

SERVES 6

Bliny are a distinctly Russian dish. They are a bit like griddlecakes or crêpes, and even bear a close family resemblance to blintzes (see page 208), but all comparisons end there. Any smoked fish can be substituted for the mackerel. The batter takes some time to prepare. Once it is ready, it should be used immediately. Use plenty of butter.

1 cup lukewarm water

3 packages active dry yeast

1 cup buckwheat flour

4 cups plain white flour

4 cups warm milk

6 egg yolks, beaten

3 teaspoons sugar

4 cups soured cream (see page below)

1 teaspoon salt

1 pound butter, clarified and cooled

6 egg whites

2 pounds smoked mackerel

Put the lukewarm water in a shallow bowl. Sprinkle the yeast over the water. Leave it to stand for 3 minutes and then stir until the yeast is completely dissolved. Put the bowl in a warm dry place for 5 minutes.

♦ Combine the buckwheat and white flour in a large mixing bowl. Make a well in the center of the flour and the yeast. Add 2 cups of the warm milk.

♦ Stir well and then beat vigorously until the mixture is even and smooth. Cover the bowl with a clean cloth and set aside in a warm dry place for 3 hours.

♦ Remove the cloth and stir the bliny mixture vigorously. Cover the bowl again and return it to the warm dry place. Leave it to stand for 1 hour 45 minutes.

♦ Stir in the remaining milk and the egg yolks, sugar, 6 tablespoons of the soured cream, salt and 6 tablespoons of the clarified butter. Beat until the mixture is smooth.

♦ In another bowl, beat the egg whites until they are stiff. Gradually fold the egg whites into the bliny batter. Leave it to stand for 40 minutes.

♦ Preheat the oven to 250°F. Coat the bottom of a very large, heavy skillet with 4 tablespoons of the clarified butter and place over a high heat.

♦ Add 3 tablespoons of the bliny batter. Tilt the pan to coat it with a thin layer of the batter. Cook the bliny for 2 to 3 minutes on each side. When the pancake is done, transfer it to a ceramic or glass dish with a tight lid and keep warm in oven. Repeat with the remaining batter, adding more butter as needed.

♦ To serve the bliny, first brush each one with clarified butter, place a wedge of smoked mackerel on the bliny, fold it over and top with a spoonful of soured cream.

Soured Cream

MAKES 6 CUPS

Russian-style soured cream is somewhat thinner than that sold commercially. This easy recipe for homemade soured cream is close to the authentic style, and is far more flavorful than the commercial equivalent.

1½ cups buttermilk

6 cups heavy cream

Combine the buttermilk and cream in a large jar with a tightly fitting lid. Close tightly and shake vigorously for 90 seconds. Leave it to stand at room temperature for 2 days. Refrigerate for 2½ days before using.

Charlotte Russe

SERVES 8

The great French chef Antoine Carême created this celebrated dessert after visiting Russia in the mid-nineteenth century.

16 ladyfingers, halved lengthwise

4 egg yolks

½ cup sugar

1 cup milk

1 scant tablespoon pure vanilla extract

2 tablespoons unflavored gelatin, dissolved in ¼ cup cold water

½ cup soured cream

½ cup heavy cream, chilled

1 tablespoon Triple Sec liqueur

20 ounces frozen raspberries, thawed and drained

3 tablespoons superfine sugar

2 tablespoons blackberry brandy

Set 16 ladyfinger halves aside. Take the remaining ladyfingers and cut diagonal slices from each side of one end, so that one end of each is still curved and the other comes to a point.

♦ In a 1 quart pudding mold, arrange the trimmed ladyfinger halves at the bottom so that their points touch and their diagonal edges are side by side. The pattern on the bottom of the pudding mold should resemble a doily with beveled edges. Place the remaining untrimmed ladyfinger halves against the side of the mold, standing them straight up. Try not to leave any gaps between the untrimmed ladyfinger halves.

♦ In a mixing bowl, beat the egg yolks. Gradually beat in the sugar. Continue beating until the sugar is fully incorporated into the egg yolks.

♦ Warm the milk and vanilla extract in a small saucepan over a low heat. When the milk starts to bubble, beat it into the egg mixture.

♦ Pour the egg and milk mixture back into the saucepan. Cook over a low heat, stirring all the time, until the mixture becomes a thick custard. Do not let the mixture boil. Stir in the dissolved gelatin. When the mixture has an even consistency throughout, strain it through a fine sieve into a mixing bowl.

♦ In another bowl, whip the soured cream and heavy cream together until the mixture begins to stiffen.

♦ Place the bowl containing the custard mixture inside a larger bowl. Put ice cubes and cold water into the larger bowl until it comes halfway up the sides of the custard bowl. Stir the custard with a metal spoon until it begins to thicken noticeably.

♦ Fold the whipped cream mixture into the custard, breaking up any lumps with a whisk or fork. Stir in the Triple Sec liqueur.

♦ Pour the contents of the custard bowl into the mold lined with ladyfingers. Chill for 5 to 6 hours before serving.

♦ Blend the strained raspberries, superfine sugar and blackberry brandy together in a small bowl. Spoon the sauce over slices of the Charlotte Russe just before serving.

Russian Chanuka Dinner

The main course at a traditional Russian Chanuka Dinner is almost always pickled beef tongue or other pickled meat. It is also customary to end the meal with a sweet fruit dessert. Potato pancakes, however, the one dish that most Jews now associate with Chanuka, would not be served (but see page 214 for a recipe).

Hearty Beef Soup
Pickled Beef Tongue
Glazed Chicken Wings
Braised Carrots and Onions
Cucumber Salad
Fruit Kisel

♦

Hearty Beef Soup

SERVES 8

This hearty beef soup provides considerable protection from the inside out against the rigors of a severe Russian winter.

1 pound beef brisket or flank, thinly sliced

1 pound beef bones, split into pieces

1 large turnip, cut into pieces

1 onion, quartered

2 celery stalks, finely chopped

1 carrot, halved

3 tablespoons chopped green pepper

$\frac{1}{4}$ teaspoon salt

$\frac{1}{4}$ teaspoon black pepper

4 tablespoons chopped fresh chives

$\frac{1}{4}$ cup red wine

2 quarts water

$\frac{1}{2}$ pound egg noodles

Put all the ingredients except the noodles into a large soup pot. Bring to a boil, reduce the heat and simmer, tightly covered, for 5 to 6 hours. Add the noodles. Raise the heat to medium and cook for a further 12 to 15 minutes. Serve hot.

Pickled Beef Tongue

SERVES 8

To a Russian Jew of the late nineteenth century, this dish meant Chanuka.

4-5 pound smoked beef tongue

2 cups white wine vinegar

3 large onions, quartered

$\frac{3}{4}$ cup sugar

1 bay leaf

1 whole clove

$\frac{1}{4}$ teaspoon white pepper

2 tablespoons honey

$\frac{1}{4}$ teaspoon cinnamon

2 tablespoons pickling spice, tied up in cheesecloth

In a large pot, cover the smoked beef tongue with water. Bring the water to a boil. Skim off the fat that rises to the surface. Reduce the heat to low and cover the pan. Simmer for 3 to 4 hours, or until tender, depending on the size of the tongue. Remove the pot from the heat and leave the tongue to cool in the liquid. Skim off the fat.

♦ Put 3 cups of the cooking liquid into a saucepan. Discard the remaining cooking liquid or save it for stock. Add the vinegar, onions, sugar, bay leaf, clove, white pepper, honey and cinnamon. Bring the mixture to a boil and simmer for 5 minutes. Add the pickling spice. Remove the clove and simmer for a further 5 minutes. Remove the bay leaf and spice bag. Pour the liquid over the tongue. Chill for at least 90 minutes and serve.

Glazed Chicken Wings

SERVES 8

Sweet foods are traditional on Chanuka.

3 pounds chicken wings

4 tablespoons tomato sauce

$\frac{1}{2}$ teaspoon garlic powder

$\frac{1}{2}$ teaspoon onion powder

$\frac{1}{4}$ teaspoon ground ginger

$\frac{1}{4}$ teaspoon cayenne pepper

$\frac{1}{2}$ cup white wine

4 tablespoons honey

4 tablespoons apricot preserves

2 tablespoons peach preserves

Preheat the oven to 375°F. Cut the tips from the wings (discard or save them for broth). Spread the chicken wings in one layer in a large greased pan. Bake for 30 minutes.

♦ Meanwhile, mix together the tomato sauce, garlic powder, onion powder, ginger, cayenne pepper and wine in a small bowl.

♦ Spoon the mixture over the chicken wings and bake for a further 30 minutes. While the wings are cooking, mix together the honey, apricot and peach preserves in a small bowl. Brush the glaze over the chicken wings. Raise the heat to 400°F. Bake for a further 10 to 15 minutes, or until the wings are golden and glazed.

Braised Carrots and Onions

SERVES 6—8

The natural sweetness of carrots and their golden color was thought to represent good luck on festive occasions.

4 tablespoons margarine

1 medium onion, sliced into rings

$\frac{1}{4}$ cup finely chopped scallions

2 large tomatoes, cut into eighths and seeded

16 baby carrots, scraped and cut into quarters

$\frac{1}{4}$ teaspoon salt

$\frac{1}{4}$ teaspoon ground white pepper

1 tablespoon chopped fresh coriander

2 tablespoons chopped fresh parsley

Melt the margarine in a large saucepan over a low heat. Add the onion and scallions. Sauté, stirring constantly, for 5 minutes. Add the tomatoes and raise the heat to medium. Sauté, stirring constantly for a further 3 to 4 minutes.

♦ Add the carrots, salt and white pepper, coriander and parsley. Reduce the heat to low. Cook for 1 to 2 minutes stirring constantly. Cover the saucepan and reduce the heat to very low. Simmer for 5 minutes and serve.

Cucumber Salad

SERVES 8

Cucumbers or pickles feature in many Russian dishes. This salad, which is slightly wilted when served, still has a delicious crunch to it.

3 large cucumbers, peeled and thinly sliced

2 cups red wine vinegar

$\frac{1}{2}$ teaspoon celery salt

$\frac{1}{2}$ head lettuce, shredded

1 tablespoon honey

$\frac{1}{4}$ teaspoon black pepper

$\frac{1}{2}$ teaspoon fresh dill, chopped

4 tablespoons olive oil

1 teaspoon Dijon-style mustard

Toss all the ingredients thoroughly in a large salad bowl. Chill for 2 hours before serving.

Fruit Kisel

SERVES 8—10

Kisel is a cold, thick liquid dessert very popular in Russia. There are many different recipes, and there are no hard and fast rules about ingredients. Try different combinations of fruit, making sure to mash the fruit into a smooth purée. More potato starch may be needed to thicken the kisel if very juicy fresh fruits are used.

$\frac{1}{2}$ pound tart red apples, peeled, cored and cut into small chunks

$\frac{1}{4}$ pound dried apricots

$1\frac{1}{2}$ pints fresh or thawed frozen strawberries

$4\frac{1}{4}$ cups cold water

$\frac{1}{4}$ cup jellied cranberry sauce

1 cup sugar

$1\frac{1}{2}$ tablespoons potato starch, dissolved in 2 tablespoons cold water

Place the apples, apricots and strawberries in a large saucepan. Add the cranberry sauce and cold water and bring the mixture to a boil over a high heat. Reduce the heat to low and simmer uncovered for 15 minutes, stirring occasionally.

♦ With the back of a spoon, press the fruit mixture through a fine sieve into a large mixing bowl. Discard any solids that remain in the sieve. Stir in the sugar.

♦ Put the fruit and sugar mixture into a large saucepan and bring it to a boil. Reduce the heat to medium and stir in the potato starch mixture. Cook until the purée returns to a boil. Remove the saucepan from the heat and let the purée cool to room temperature.

♦ Spoon the purée into pudding or tulip glasses. Chill for 4 hours before serving.

Russian Dinner

*This average weekday meal consists of only five courses, a very small
number in the heyday of Russian Jewish cuisine.*

Sorrel and Kidney Soup
Fried Spinach
Stuffed Veal Shoulder
Merchant's Spiced Potatoes
Strawberry Peach Sherbet

Sorrel and Kidney Soup

SERVES 6—8

Kidneys, which have lost some of their attraction in modern times, were considered a delicacy by most Slavs and Europeans. They are shown at their best in this traditional Russian soup.

4 tablespoons margarine

1 cup small onions, quartered

1 cup chopped celery

1 large dill pickle, finely chopped

$\frac{1}{2}$ cup finely chopped parsley

$1\frac{1}{2}$ pounds fresh sorrel leaves, stemmed and chopped

$\frac{1}{2}$ pound fresh spinach, coarsely chopped

1 teaspoon salt

1 teaspoon black pepper

8 cups chicken broth

1 pound veal kidneys

$\frac{1}{4}$ cup flour

2 tablespoons olive oil

2 egg yolks, beaten

In a large casserole, melt 3 tablespoons of the margarine. Reduce the heat to low and stir in the onions and celery. Cover and simmer for 8 minutes.

◆ Add the pickle, parsley, sorrel, spinach, salt and pepper. Stir and cook over a low heat for 2 minutes. Add the chicken broth and raise the heat to high. Bring the mixture to a boil. Reduce the heat and simmer for 25 minutes.

◆ While the stock simmers, trim the fat off the kidneys and cut them crosswise into $\frac{1}{2}$ inch thick slices. Dredge the slices lightly in the flour.

◆ Heat the remaining tablespoon of margarine and the olive oil in a large, heavy skillet over a medium heat. When the mixture begins to brown, add the kidney slices. Sauté, stirring constantly, for 4 to 6 minutes, or until the slices are browned. Add the kidney slices to the stock and simmer for 10 minutes.

◆ Add the egg yolks to the soup, stirring constantly. Simmer for a further 3 minutes and serve.

Fried Spinach

SERVES 6—8

This novel way to prepare fresh spinach originated in Riga. It is popular with Jews throughout Russia and the Ukraine. It should only be made with fresh spinach.

3 tablespoons peanut oil

2 garlic cloves, diced

1 small onion, finely chopped

2 pounds fresh spinach, thoroughly washed and shredded

$\frac{1}{4}$ cup white wine

$\frac{1}{4}$ teaspoon salt

Heat the oil in a large, heavy skillet. Add the garlic and onion and sauté, stirring constantly, over a moderate heat for 2 minutes.

◆ Reduce the heat to low. Add the spinach, wine and salt. Cook, stirring constantly, until the spinach is wilted and bright green, about 3 minutes.

Stuffed Veal Shoulder

SERVES 6—8

This succulent entrée combines the flavor of three different meats. It's a good dish for any religious or secular holiday meal.

1 pound ground veal

1 pound lean ground beef

½ pound ground chicken

½ cup finely chopped onion

¼ cup finely chopped scallions

½ cup soft breadcrumbs

2 cups cold water

2 eggs

1 teaspoon salt

½ teaspoon white pepper

4-5 pounds veal shoulder, boned

1 garlic clove, crushed

4 hard-boiled eggs

6 tablespoons margarine

In a large mixing bowl, combine the ground veal, ground beef, ground chicken, onion, scallions, breadcrumbs, water, eggs, salt and pepper. Mix thoroughly until the stuffing has an even consistency.

♦ Preheat the oven to 375°F.

♦ With a sharp knife, cut the veal shoulder almost in half horizontally, where it is thickest. The veal shoulder should lie flat on a large cutting board. Rub the cut surface of the veal with the garlic clove and then cover it with a large piece of waxed paper. Beat the veal with a meat pounder until the meat is flattened.

♦ Remove the paper and spread half the flattened veal shoulder with half the stuffing mixture. Arrange the hard-boiled eggs on top of the stuffing. Spread the remaining stuffing mixture over the eggs.

♦ Fold the veal over and tie with strong kitchen twine at 2 inch intervals.

♦ Place the veal in a shallow roasting pan filled with 2 inches water. Roast for 2 hours. Remove the veal from the oven. Remove the roast from the pan and put it on a carving board. Cut and remove the string. Let the roast stand for 10 minutes before slicing.

♦ Melt the margarine in a small saucepan. Add the drippings from the roasting pan. Stir well and simmer for 10 minutes, uncovered, until the gravy is slightly reduced and thickened. Serve the gravy separately.

Merchant's Spiced Potatoes

SERVES 6—8

This traditional Russian dish shows a pronounced Eastern influence. It uses spices that at one time only a merchant could afford.

2 tablespoons vegetable oil

$\frac{1}{2}$ teaspoon dry mustard

1 tomato, seeded and finely chopped

4 tablespoons green pepper, diced

$\frac{1}{4}$ teaspoon cayenne pepper

$\frac{1}{4}$ teaspoon ground turmeric

$\frac{1}{4}$ teaspoon ground allspice

$\frac{1}{4}$ teaspoon ground ginger

$\frac{1}{4}$ teaspoon salt

$\frac{1}{2}$ teaspoon sugar

$\frac{1}{4}$ teaspoon ground coriander

5 large boiled potatoes, cut into chunks

Heat the oil in a large, heavy skillet over a moderate heat. Add the mustard, tomato, green pepper, cayenne pepper, turmeric, allspice, ginger, salt, sugar and coriander. Cook, stirring constantly, for 2 minutes.

♦ Add the potatoes and cook, stirring constantly, until the potatoes are coated with the spices and heated through, about 5 minutes.

Strawberry Peach Sherbet

SERVES 6—8

Fruit sherbets, which were perfected by the Austrians, quickly became a favorite dessert among the Russian Jews. Since sherbets contain no milk, they can be served with either dairy or meat meals.

4 large peaches

2 cups fresh strawberries, chopped

$\frac{1}{4}$ cup fresh lemon juice

$\frac{3}{4}$ cup superfine sugar

Bring 3 cups water to a boil in a medium-sized pot. Add the peaches and cook for 2 minutes.

♦ Remove the peaches from the pot and drain well. When the peaches are cool enough to handle, remove the skins and pits. Mash the peaches into a pulp in a large mixing bowl.

♦ Purée the peach pulp, strawberries and lemon juice in a liquidizer or food processor.

♦ Stir the sugar into the fruit mixture and purée for another 10 to 15 seconds. Pour the mixture into a large, shallow dish and freeze until hard. Remove the dish from the freezer 1 hour before serving and let the sherbet soften in the refrigerator.

Russian Dairy Lunch

This four-course Russian dairy lunch features two Russian specialties: a flaky salmon loaf and a borscht, Moscow-style.

Moscow Borscht
Vegetables in Vinaigrette
Salmon Loaf
Apple Charlotte

♦

Moscow Borscht

SERVES 8

Where there are Russians, there is borscht — hot or cold, with or without sausages, with or without beef broth. The variations on the theme are almost endless. This deliciously light and flavorful dairy variation calls for swordfish meat and vegetable broth.

3 tablespoons butter

$\frac{1}{2}$ cup chopped onion

8 cups vegetable broth

2 pounds red beets, peeled and cut into $\frac{1}{4}$ inch rounds

$\frac{1}{4}$ cup chopped scallions

3 tablespoons lemon juice

$\frac{1}{4}$ cup red wine vinegar

1 large swordfish steak, cubed

1 teaspoon salt

$\frac{1}{2}$ teaspoon white pepper

$\frac{1}{4}$ cup white wine

4 sprigs of parsley

1 bay leaf

2 cups white cabbage, shredded

2 tomatoes, peeled, seeded and chopped

$\frac{1}{2}$ cup finely chopped fresh dill

soured cream

In a large soup pot, melt the butter over a moderate heat. Add the chopped onions and sauté until they are browned, about 4 to 5 minutes. Add the vegetable broth, beets, scallions, lemon juice, vinegar, swordfish cubes, salt and white pepper. Simmer for 25 minutes.

♦ Add the white wine, parsley, bay leaf, cabbage, tomatoes and dill. Reduce the heat to low and simmer for a further 50 minutes.

♦ Swirl a tablespoon of soured cream into each bowl and serve.

Vegetables in Vinaigrette

SERVES 8

1 pound fresh asparagus

1 large head fresh broccoli, cut into flowerettes

1 large can artichoke hearts, drained

For the dressing:

$\frac{1}{2}$ cup red wine vinegar

$\frac{1}{4}$ cup olive oil

2 tablespoons chopped scallions

2 tablespoons Dijon-style mustard

$\frac{1}{2}$ teaspoon dried chives

2 tablespoons honey

$\frac{1}{2}$ teaspoon celery salt

$\frac{1}{4}$ teaspoon black pepper

$\frac{1}{4}$ teaspoon ground white pepper

1 garlic clove, finely chopped

Cook the asparagus in a large, covered pot of boiling water until they are tender, about 10 to 12 minutes. Cook the broccoli flowerettes in a large pot of boiling water until they are tender but still crisp, about 7 minutes. Drain well.

♦ Put the asparagus, broccoli and artichoke hearts into a large bowl, cover and chill for 40 minutes.

♦ In another bowl, combine the vinegar, olive oil, scallions, mustard, chives, honey, salt, black pepper, white pepper and garlic. Mix well. Chill for 40 minutes.

♦ Stir the dressing well and pour it over the vegetables.

Salmon Loaf

SERVES 8

5 cups flour

$\frac{1}{2}$ pound unsalted butter, softened

8 tablespoons vegetable shortening

2 teaspoons salt

1 cup iced water

2 pounds fresh salmon, skinned and boned

4 cups cabbage, shredded

$1\frac{1}{2}$ cups roughly chopped onion

1 teaspoon black pepper

$1\frac{1}{2}$ cups white wine

1 pound mushrooms, quartered

2 egg yolks

1 cup chicken broth

4 tablespoons lemon juice

4 tablespoons chopped fresh dill

4 hard-boiled eggs, chopped

2 tablespoons sugar

In a large mixing bowl, combine the flour, $\frac{3}{4}$ cup butter, vegetable shortening and 1 teaspoon salt. Mix together with a wooden spoon until the dough has a flaky texture. Add the iced water and mix until smooth. Divide the dough into 2 equal portions. Wrap each half in plastic wrap and refrigerate for $3\frac{1}{2}$ hours.

♦ Put the salmon, remaining butter, cabbage, onion, pepper, wine, mushrooms, remaining salt, egg yolks, chicken broth, lemon juice, dill and sugar into a large saucepan. Simmer for 1 hour, or until most of the liquid has evaporated.

♦ Flake the salmon with a fork. Stir gently and add the chopped hard-boiled eggs. Stir gently again. Set the mixture aside.

♦ Roll out half the chilled dough on a lightly-floured surface into a rectangle about 1 inch thick. Dust with flour, and then roll the dough out into a sheet $\frac{1}{8}$ inch thick. Trim the sheet into a rectangle 8 × 16 inches. Repeat with the remaining dough, but trim the sheet to 10 × 16 inches.

♦ Place the smaller dough rectangle on a large, greased baking sheet. Arrange the salmon filling evenly over the dough sheet, leaving a 1 inch border around the edges. Place the larger dough sheet over the filling. Press the edges of the top and bottom dough sheets together with a fork. Chill for 15 minutes.

♦ Preheat the oven to 400°F. Bake the loaf for 1 hour. Serve immediately.

Apple Charlotte

SERVES 8

There are many kinds of charlotte. Apple charlotte, one of the simpler versions, is popular as a lunchtime dish.

2 tablespoons unsalted butter, softened
$1\frac{1}{2}$ cups unsalted butter, clarified
12 large slices of white bread, halved, crusts removed
3 pounds tart apples, peeled, cored and chopped
3 pounds sweet apples, peeled, cored and chopped
$1\frac{1}{2}$ cups sugar
$\frac{1}{2}$ cup water
2 tablespoons lime juice
2 tablespoons lemon juice
1 teaspoon cinnamon
2 cups apricot preserves
$\frac{1}{4}$ cup apricot brandy
$\frac{1}{4}$ cup orange juice
$\frac{1}{4}$ teaspoon pure vanilla extract

Rub the softened butter over the inside surface of a pudding mold.

♦ Put the clarified butter into a large mixing bowl. Dip the bread into the butter and line the sides and bottom of the pudding mold with them.

♦ Combine the apples, sugar, water, lemon juice and lime juice in a large flameproof casserole. Bring the mixture to a boil, cover and simmer for 40 minutes over a low heat. Add the cinnamon and cook, uncovered, over a medium heat for a further 15 minutes. Chill the mixture for 1 hour.

♦ Gently pour the chilled apple mixture into the prepared pudding mold.

♦ Preheat the oven to 400°F. Bake the pudding for 1 hour. Cool for 30 minutes at room temperature.

♦ Invert the pudding on a large flat plate. Gently shake the mold to loosen the apple charlotte. Carefully pull the pudding mold away.

♦ In a small mixing bowl, combine the apricot preserves, apricot brandy, orange juice and vanilla extract. Spoon over the apple charlotte before serving.

Polish Yom Kippur

Yom Kippur, or the Day of Atonement, is a solemn fast day. A boiled dinner of several different specialties often used to be served before the holy day began.

Beef Chopped Liver
Chicken in the Pot with Soup
Kreplach
Matzoh Balls
Boiled Beef
Baked Apples

Beef Chopped Liver

SERVES 8

A variation on the more familiar chicken chopped liver, this recipe is a specialty of the Eastern European Jews

½ cup beef stock
1 pound fresh calf's liver, cubed
1 garlic clove, finely chopped
1 pound fresh chicken livers, halved
2 hard-boiled eggs, finely chopped
½ cup mayonnaise
¼ cup diced green pepper
1 large celery stalk, finely chopped
¼ cup diced onions
2 tablespoons sherry
1 teaspoon brandy
2 tablespoons unflavored dry breadcrumbs
½ teaspoon salt
1 teaspoon white pepper

Heat the beef broth in a medium-sized saucepan. Add the liver cubes and garlic and cook, stirring frequently, for 10 to 12 minutes, or until the liver is thoroughly cooked. Remove the liver cubes and set them aside. Discard the cooking liquid.
♦ Put the chicken livers in a saucepan and add enough cold water to cover. Bring the liquid to a boil and cook for 15 minutes, or until the livers are thoroughly cooked. Drain well.
♦ Put the calf's liver cubes, chicken livers, eggs, mayonnise, green pepper, celery, onions, sherry, brandy, breadcrumbs, salt and white pepper into a large mixing bowl. Mash the ingredients together with a fork until the mixture has a fine and even consistency. Cover the bowl and refrigerate for at least 2 hours before serving.

Chicken in the Pot with Soup

SERVES 6—8

This dish, the queen of all chicken soups, is served with kreplach and matzoh balls. The kreplach, matzoh balls and fine egg noodles should be prepared separately and combined just before serving.

2 large parsley sprigs
1 large parsnip
1 small leek
1 dill sprig
3½ quarts water
2 celery stalks, halved
2 large onions, halved
5 carrots, halved
3 pound chicken, cut into pieces
1 teaspoon salt
½ teaspoon black pepper
¼ teaspoon ground white pepper
1 cup fine egg noodles

Tie the parsley, parsnip, leek and dill together with kitchen string.

♦ Fill a large soup pot with the water. Add the bunch of vegetables and herbs and the celery, onions, carrots and chicken pieces. Bring the liquid to a boil. Add the salt, black pepper and white pepper. Reduce the heat to low. Simmer for 1 hour 45 minutes.

♦ Remove and discard the bunch of vegetables and herbs. Add the egg noodles to the pot. Simmer for 10 minutes, stirring occasionally.

♦ Serve the soup with the vegetables and chicken pieces in large deep bowls.

Kreplach

MAKES ABOUT 50 KREPLACH

Kreplach in chicken soup are traditionally served on Purim and during Succoth, as well as at Yom Kippur Dinner.

2 pounds boneless chuck steak, coarsely ground
4 small onions, coarsely chopped
5 tablespoons vegetable oil
$\frac{1}{2}$ teaspoon salt
$\frac{1}{2}$ teaspoon black pepper
2 cups fine wholemeal flour
2 eggs
$1\frac{1}{2}$ cups warm water

In a large saucepan, brown the meat and onions in the oil over a low heat for 8 to 10 minutes. Add $\frac{1}{4}$ teaspoon salt and the black pepper. Stir well. Remove from the heat and set aside.

♦ In a large mixing bowl, make the flour into a mound. Make a well in the flour. Sprinkle the remaining salt over the flour and break the eggs into the well. Beat with a whisk, gradually adding the warm water, until the consistency of the dough is smooth and even. Roll the dough into a ball.

♦ Cut the dough into approximately 15 equal pieces. One by one, roll each piece out into a thin sheet. Cut 3, 3 inch rounds from each sheet with a cookie cutter. Repeat the process until all the dough is used up.

♦ Place 1 teaspoon of the meat and onion filling in the center of each dough round. Fold the dough over and seal the edges together with the blunt end of a spoon.

♦ Bring a very large pot of water to the boil. Drop in the kreplach, about 8 to 15 at a time, depending on the size of the pot. When the water returns to the boil, cook the kreplach for 3 to 5 minutes, or until they float to the top. Remove with a slotted spoon and set aside. If the kreplach are not being served within 30 minutes, refrigerate them. Add them to the chicken in the pot soup for 4 minutes before serving.

Matzoh Balls

SERVES 8

Also called knaidlach, matzoh balls are not just served for Passover.

4 eggs, separated
2 cups matzoh meal
$\frac{1}{2}$ teaspoon ground ginger
$\frac{1}{2}$ teaspoon ground white pepper
$\frac{1}{2}$ teaspoon salt
5 tablespoons chicken fat
1 cup hot chicken broth
4 quarts water

Beat the egg whites in a medium-sized mixing bowl until stiff. Set aside.
♦ In a large mixing bowl, combine the matzoh meal, ginger, pepper, and salt. Add the fat, broth and egg yolks. Fold in the egg whites and chill for 90 minutes.
♦ In a large soup pot, bring the water to a boil. Form the matzoh meal dough into balls with a diameter of about 1½ inches and drop them into the pot. Cover tightly and cook for 25 to 30 minutes. Do not remove the cover during this time. If the matzoh balls are not being used within 30 minutes, refrigerate them and add them to the chicken in the pot soup 5 minutes before serving.

Boiled Beef

SERVES 8

This substantial dish is remarkably simple to prepare. The method is ideal for making less expensive beef cuts tender and flavorful.

3 pounds beef flank
2 cups beef broth
2 cups chicken broth
2 cups white wine
3 large onions, quartered
1 parsley sprig
2 bay leaves
6 potatoes, peeled and quartered
4 large carrots, peeled and halved
1 pound green beans, trimmed and halved
5 small beets, peeled and quartered
1 large turnip, peeled and cubed
1 garlic clove, crushed
½ teaspoon salt
½ teaspoon black pepper

Put all the ingredients into a large, heavy pan. Simmer, covered, over a medium heat for 1 hour. Reduce the heat to low and simmer for 1 hour longer.
♦ Remove the beef from the pan and leave it to stand for 10 minutes before slicing. Serve the beef slices in bowls with the vegetables and broth ladled over them.

Baked Apples

SERVES 8

Although they are always called baked, the apples in this light dessert are steamed.

8 large red baking apples
4 whole cloves
1 teaspoon cinnamon
2 teaspoons sugar
2 teaspoons brown sugar
8 tablespoons honey

Place 4 apples into each of two large pans with 2 cups cold water. Add 2 cloves, ½ teaspoon cinnamon, 1 teaspoon sugar, 1 teaspoon brown sugar and 4 tablespoons honey to each saucepan.
♦ Cover, and steam the apples for 5 minutes over a medium heat. Remove the cloves and steam for a further 5 minutes. Let the apples cool in their liquid for 10 to 15 minutes. Serve warm, with some of the cooking liquid spooned over each apple. The apples can also be chilled and served cold.

Polish Succoth Dinner

Succoth celebrates the harvest. In ancient Palestine, the harvesters would build booths (succoth) in the fields and spend the night in them. Today many observant Jews still build a succah every year and at least eat dinner in it. Among the Polish Jews, the meal would be one with pungent, earthy flavors, what the Poles idiomatically call tam (pronounced 'tohm'). Braised country foods are traditional. So is the famous version of stuffed cabbage, perhaps because cabbage is abundant at harvest time.

Little Meatballs
Garlic Chicken Soup
Baal Shem Tov's Soup
Polish Stuffed Cabbage
Holiday Carrots
Berry Kuchen

Little Meatballs

SERVES 8

This classic Polish dish is often served on holidays. Unlike most of the recipes in this book, where there is a wide latitude for variation, this recipe should be followed exactly. Good quality beef chuck steak is recommended for best results.

> 2 pounds beef chuck steak, ground
>
> 2 cups chicken broth
>
> $\frac{1}{4}$ cup tomato paste
>
> $\frac{1}{4}$ cup grape jelly
>
> $\frac{1}{2}$ teaspoon salt
>
> $\frac{1}{4}$ teaspoon ground white pepper
>
> 1 garlic clove, finely chopped
>
> $\frac{1}{4}$ teaspoon dried oregano
>
> $\frac{1}{4}$ teaspoon dried rosemary
>
> 2 tablespoons chicken fat
>
> $\frac{1}{2}$ teaspoon dried dill
>
> $\frac{1}{2}$ teaspoon dried basil

In a large mixing bowl combine the ground beef, tomato paste, $\frac{1}{2}$ cup of the chicken broth, grape jelly, salt, white pepper, garlic, oregano and rosemary. Mix well. Shape the mixture into meatballs approximately 1 inch in diameter.

♦ In a large saucepan, melt the chicken fat over a low heat. Add the meatballs and brown for 5 minutes. Add the remaining chicken broth and the dill and basil. Simmer for 15 minutes over a very low heat. Serve warm.

Garlic Chicken Soup

SERVES 8

The simple yet pungent flavor of this traditional country soup was thought to arouse the taste buds for the courses to follow. This recipe can be traced back at least as far as the seventeenth century.

> $1\frac{1}{2}$ quarts chicken broth
>
> $\frac{1}{4}$ cup white wine
>
> 1 pound boned, skinned and shredded chicken
>
> $1\frac{1}{2}$ cups peeled and quartered garlic cloves
>
> $\frac{1}{2}$ cup chopped onion
>
> 1 tablespoon chopped scallions

Combine the chicken broth, white wine and shredded chicken meat in a medium-sized saucepan. Simmer over a low heat for 15 minutes.

♦ Add the garlic cloves, chopped onions and scallions to the soup. Simmer for 10 to 12 minutes longer and serve. This soup is especially good with chunks of crusty French bread.

Baal Shem Tov's Soup

SERVES 8

The Baal Shem Tov (Master of the Good Name) was Israel ben Eliezer (1700—60), the founder of Hassidism. Much legend surrounds his life, but we know that he was an orphan and that he was not very well educated. This bean soup is said to have been a favorite of his.

3 tablespoons chicken fat

2 onions, chopped

1 cup chopped celery

2 parsley sprigs

1 bay leaf

½ teaspoon dried thyme

1 beef soup bone

6 cups cooked black turtle beans

6 cups beef broth

4 cups fl oz water

salt to taste

black pepper to taste

4 tablespoons brandy

2 tablespoons lemon juice

Melt the chicken fat in a large pot. Add the onions, celery, parsley, bay leaf and thyme. Cook over a low heat, stirring occasionally, for 10 minutes. Add the beef bone, beans, beef broth, water, salt and pepper. Bring the liquid to a boil, reduce the heat, and simmer for 3 hours. Add more water if needed.

◊ Remove and discard the beef bone, parsley sprigs and bay leaf. Add the brandy and lemon juice and stir well. Add more water if necessary.

Polish Stuffed Cabbage

SERVES 8

This distinctly Polish variation on a traditional Jewish dish differs slightly from the Russian version. It is sure to delight all stuffed cabbage devotees.

1 large head white cabbage
1 pound ground beef sirloin
$\frac{1}{2}$ pound ground veal
$\frac{1}{2}$ pound lean ground lamb
3 medium-sized onions, chopped
2 garlic cloves, finely chopped
2 egg yolks
1 cup coarsely chopped fresh parsley
$\frac{1}{2}$ teaspoon ground white pepper
3 tablespoons tomato paste
$1\frac{1}{2}$ teaspoon salt
2 large carrots, very finely chopped
1 cup apple sauce
$\frac{1}{2}$ cup golden seedless raisins
$\frac{1}{4}$ cup apricot preserves
16 ounces tomato sauce
5 tomatoes, deseeded and mashed
3 tablespoons brown sugar
2 tablespoons white wine vinegar
$\frac{1}{2}$ teaspoon black pepper

Remove and discard the tough outer cabbage leaves. With a sharp knife, core the cabbage. Cook the cabbage in a large pot of boiling water with $\frac{1}{2}$ teaspoon of the salt for 5 minutes. Remove the cabbage and peel off all the outer leaves that will come away easily without tearing. Return the cabbage to the boiling water, remove after another 5 minutes and repeat the process of removing softened cabbage leaves. Repeat until you have 20 to 25 whole softened cabbage leaves. Finely dice any remaining cabbage and set it aside for use in the sauce.

♦ In a large mixing bowl, combine the ground sirloin, veal, and lamb. Add one of the chopped onions, the garlic, egg yolks, half of the chopped parsley, the white pepper, tomato paste and $\frac{1}{2}$ teaspoon salt. Mix the stuffing thoroughly.

♦ To make the sauce, combine the remaining salt, onions and parsley, the diced cabbage leaves, and the carrots, apple sauce, raisins, apricot preserves, tomato sauce, tomatoes, brown sugar, vinegar and black pepper in a medium-sized saucepan. Stir over a low heat until well blended. Cover and simmer for 10 minutes over a very low heat.

♦ Place 2 tablespoons of the stuffing in the center of each softened cabbage leaf. Bring the end of the cabbage leaf towards the center, and then roll it over. Fold the cabbage leaf ends under so that the cabbage package is completely sealed. Repeat until all the cabbage leaves are stuffed and rolled. Save any remaining stuffing to add to the sauce.

♦ Preheat the oven to 350°F. Place the cabbage rolls side-by-side in 2 layers in a large saucepan. Pour the sauce, including any leftover stuffing, over the cabbage rolls. Cover and bake for 2 hours.

Holiday Carrots

SERVES 8

In addition to being a traditional on Succoth, this dish is also often served on Purim.

$1\frac{1}{2}$ pounds baby carrots, cut into small pieces

1 cup canned mandarin orange sections, drained

$\frac{1}{4}$ cup wataer

2 tablespoons margarine

$\frac{1}{4}$ cup fresh lime juice

$\frac{1}{4}$ teaspoon salt

Place all the ingredients in a large wooden chopping bowl. Chop finely.
♦ Put the mixture into a medium-sized saucepan and simmer over a low heat for 20 minutes. Serve hot.

Berry Kuchen

SERVES 8

Borrowed from the German-Austrian Jews, this festive dessert is a delicious way to end a meal.

2 cups flour

$\frac{1}{2}$ teaspoon salt

$\frac{3}{4}$ cup unsalted margarine

2 tablespoons lemon juice

$1\frac{1}{4}$ cups superfine sugar

$\frac{1}{2}$ teaspoon pure vanilla extract

$\frac{1}{4}$ teaspoon ground cinnamon

1 cup fresh or frozen blueberries

1 cup fresh or frozen strawberries

1 cup fresh or frozen raspberries

If using frozen berries, thaw them completely and drain well.
♦ Preheat the oven to 375°F. In a large mixing bowl combine the flour, salt, margarine and lemon juice. Mix until the dough has an even consistency.
♦ Spread the dough mixture evenly in a 12 inch square baking dish.
♦ Combine the sugar, vanilla extract, berries and cinnamon in a mixing bowl. Mix well. Spoon the berry mixture into the baking dish on top of the dough. Bake for 1 hour 10 minutes. Serve warm.

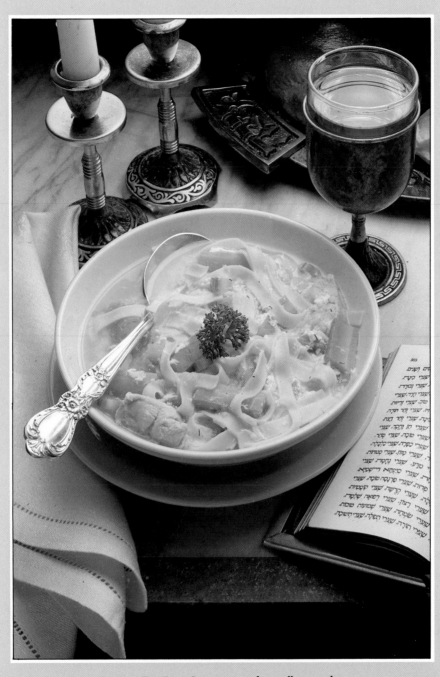

*Russian Egg Drop Soup was traditionally served as
part of a Russian Sabbath Dinner (page 61).*

Kasha ABOVE LEFT is a traditional Russian dish
made with buckwheat groats, mushrooms and
onions (page 64).

◆

Braised Carrots ABOVE RIGHT symbolized good luck
at a Russian Chanuka Dinner (page 70).

◆

Merchant's Spiced Potatoes BELOW is a Russian
dish with strong Eastern influences (page 75).

Moscow Borscht ABOVE is a variation of the most
famous of all Russian dishes (page 77).

♦

Baked Apples BELOW provide a light finish to a
Polish Yom Kippur Dinner (page 83).

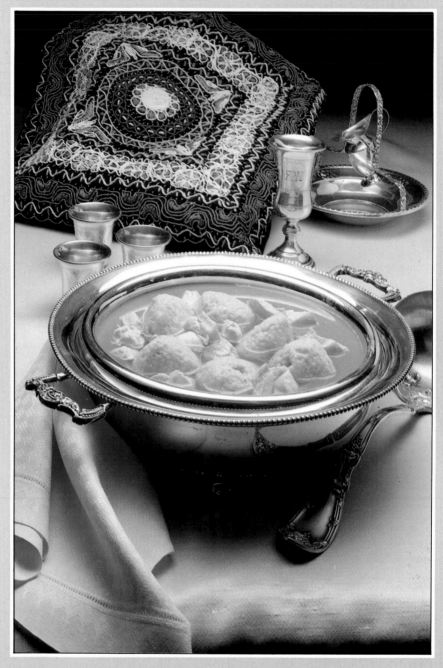

Chicken in the Pot with Soup ABOVE *is served with
Kreplach and Matzoh Balls at a Polish Yom
Kippur Dinner (page 83).*

♦

Garlic Chicken Soup ABOVE (OPPOSITE) *is a Polish
country soup dating back to the 17th century
(page 85).*

♦

Scholar's Vegetable Soup BELOW (OPPOSITE) *is
thought to have been favored by Talmudic scholars
(page 98).*

Polish Herring Salad ABOVE (OPPOSITE) *combines the piquancy of herrings with the sweetness of pears (page 99).*

◆

Lesco ABOVE *is a traditional Hungarian first course (page 102).*

◆

Cold Cherry Soup BELOW (OPPOSITE) *is an unusual Hungarian soup (page 102).*

New Potatoes with Wine ABOVE LEFT makes a
delicious accompaniment to Beef Goulash
(page 104).

◆

Kohlrabi Chicken Soup ABOVE RIGHT is a
traditional first course at a Hungarian Holiday
Supper (page 107).

◆

Chicken Paprikash BELOW is a perfect centerpiece
for a Hungarian Holiday Dinner (page 107).

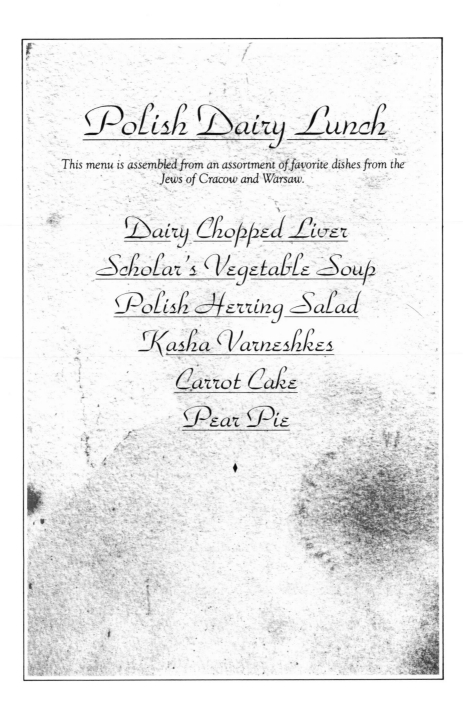

Polish Dairy Lunch

*This menu is assembled from an assortment of favorite dishes from the
Jews of Cracow and Warsaw.*

Dairy Chopped Liver
Scholar's Vegetable Soup
Polish Herring Salad
Kasha Varneshkes
Carrot Cake
Pear Pie

Dairy 'Chopped Liver'

SERVES 6

The search for the perfect meatless substitute for chopped liver to be served at dairy meals has continued for the last 150 years. The recipe below is a very acceptable version, but as experienced Jewish cooks know, the search for the ultimate recipe goes on.

1 cup chickpeas, cooked and drained

1 cup red kidney beans, cooked and drained

1 hard-boiled egg, finely chopped

$\frac{1}{2}$ cup canned mackerel fillets in tomato sauce

$\frac{1}{2}$ cup finely chopped onion

$\frac{1}{4}$ cup finely chopped celery

$\frac{1}{4}$ cup slivered carrot

2 tablespoons lemon juice

1 tablespoon red wine

Combine all the ingredients in a large wooden chopping bowl. Mash them into a paste with a fine and even consistency.

♦ Spoon the mixture into a serving bowl. Cover and chill for at least 2 hours. Serve with crackers, dark bread or on a bed of lettuce.

Scholar's Vegetable Soup

SERVES 6—8

Legend has it that Talmudic scholars, who wanted a pure diet and abstained from meat, favored this traditional Polish-Jewish vegetable soup.

1 pound ripe tomatoes, seeded and finely chopped

4 large carrots, peeled and quartered

2 cups chopped celery

3 leeks, cut into sections

1 cup fresh green peas

$\frac{1}{2}$ cup dried lentils

1 teaspoon salt

1 small head cauliflower, cut into flowerettes

1 bay leaf

$\frac{1}{2}$ teaspoon black pepper

1 tablespoon diced green pepper

4 quarts water

1 large Spanish onion, halved

2 cubes vegetable bouillon

Combine all the ingredients in a large soup pot. Bring to a boil, reduce the heat to medium and simmer for 3 hours, stirring occasionally. Serve in large soup bowls.

Polish Herring Salad

SERVES 6 — 8

This piquant salad features the addition of pear sections. Herring is something of a treat for Westernized Jews today, but at one time it was an every-day food, especially among the poor.

3 cups beets, cooked and diced

3 cups new potatoes, cooked and diced

2 cups canned pear sections, drained and cut into small pieces

32 ounces bottled herring pieces, drained

2 cups finely diced onion

1 cup red wine vinegar

$\frac{1}{2}$ teaspoon black pepper

$\frac{1}{4}$ teaspoon salt

1 cup quartered mushrooms

2 cups soured cream

$\frac{1}{2}$ cup white wine

Toss all the ingredients together in a large mixing bowl. Cover and chill for at least 3 hours before serving.

Kasha Varneshkes

SERVES 6

Kasha is a staple food throughout Russia and the Slavic countries. The variations are endless. Only use bow-tie pasta shapes; any other pasta shape won't taste right. The dish will still be authentic (perhaps more so) if $\frac{1}{2}$ cup of sliced mushrooms are added with the onions.

1 cup medium-grain kasha(buckwheat groats)

1 egg

4 tablespoons margarine or chicken fat

2 onions, diced

2 cups boiling water

salt to taste

8 ounces pasta bow-ties

Beat the egg in a bowl and add the kasha. Stir well to coat the kasha.

♦ Heat a large heavy pot on the stove top. Add the kasha and cook, stirring, until each kasha grain is dry and separate. Make sure this is done thoroughly or the kasha will be soggy and lumpy.

♦ Melt 1 tablespoon of the margarine in a small skillet. Add the onions and sauté until soft.

♦ Add the onions, boiling water, remaining margarine and salt to taste to the kasha. Cover tightly and cook over a medium heat until all the water has been absorbed, about 40 minutes.

♦ Cook the pasta in a large pot of boiling water until it is cooked *al dente*. Drain well. Mix the pasta with the kasha and serve.

Carrot Cake

MAKES 1 CAKE

In Warsaw just before World War I, this cake was a favorite among café-goers seeking to emulate their Parisian counterparts.

3 cups flour

3 cups sugar

3 teaspoons baking soda

2 teaspoons ground cinnamon

1 teaspoon pure vanilla extract

1½ cups vegetable oil

6 eggs

5 carrots, finely grated

½ teaspoon salt

1 cup golden seedless raisins

½ cup slivered apple

Preheat the oven to 350°F. Mix all the ingredients together in a large mixing bowl until the consistency is even.

◆ Grease a 9 × 15 inch cake pan and pour in the batter. Bake for 40 minutes, or until a cocktail stick inserted into the center of the cake comes out dry.

Pear Pie

SERVES 6 — 8

Pears are a favourite fruit in Eastern Europe.

singlecrust 9 inch pie shell

5 tablespoons superfine sugar

1 tablespoon flour

1 teaspoon nutmeg

6 ripe pears, peeled, cored and sliced

1 teaspoon grated orange rind

4 tablespoons chopped golden seedless raisins

2 tablespoons lemon juice

2 tablespoons sweet white wine

2 tablespoons vegetable oil

½ cup heavy cream

Preheat the oven to 400°F.

◆ Line a 9 inch pie plate with the pastry. Prick the pastry with a fork and sprinkle it with 2 tablespoons of the sugar, flour and nutmeg. Arrange the pear slices in the pastry and sprinkle them with the orange rind and chopped raisins. Combine the lemon juice, wine and vegetable oil in a bowl and mix well. Pour the mixture over the pear slices.

◆ Put the remaining sugar and cream in a bowl. Stir until all the sugar is dissolved. Pour the mixture over the pear slices.

◆ Bake the pie for 12 minutes. Reduce the heat to 350°F and bake for 25 minutes. Serve warm.

Hungarian Jewish Supper

*This meal of traditional Hungarian dishes is built around a main course
of beef goulash, a staple of Hungarian cuisine.*

Lesco
Cold Cherry Soup
Beef Goulash
Asparagus with Nutmeg
New Potatoes with Wine
Walnut Apricot Pancakes

♦

Lesco

SERVES 6—8

This traditional Hungarian appetizer is similar to a ragoût.

5 tablespoons chicken fat

1 cup finely chopped onion

2 garlic cloves, chopped

2 pounds ripe tomatoes, skinned, seeded and coarsely chopped

$1\frac{1}{2}$ pounds green peppers, seeded and cut into strips

$\frac{1}{2}$ teaspoon salt

1 teaspoon black pepper

3 tablespoons sweet Hungarian paprika

$\frac{1}{4}$ cup black olives, pitted and diced

1 cup tomato paste

$1\frac{1}{2}$ pounds kosher beef sausage, thinly sliced

6—8 eggs

Melt the chicken fat in a large saucepan. Add the onions and garlic and cook for 10—12 minutes over a low heat.

♦ Add the tomatoes, green peppers, salt, pepper, paprika and olives. Turn the heat up to medium, cover, and cook for 15 minutes.

♦ Add the tomato paste and sausage. Reduce the heat to low and simmer the lesco, covered, for 30 minutes.

♦ After the lesco has cooked for 25 minutes, fry the eggs on both sides until the whites are firm. Serve the lesco in soup bowls, topping each portion with a fried egg.

Cold Cherry Soup

SERVES 8

This unusual soup is made using both sour and black cherries and is served cold.

4 cups cold water

$1\frac{1}{2}$ cups sugar

$\frac{1}{4}$ teaspoon ground cinnamon

3 cups fresh or canned sour red cherries, pitted

3 cups fresh or canned black cherries, pitted

2 tablespoons lemon juice

1 cup red wine

$\frac{1}{4}$ teaspoon dried dill

$\frac{1}{4}$ teaspoon ground white pepper

2 tablespoons water, at room temperature

1 tablespoon arrowroot

In a medium-sized saucepan, combine all the ingredients except the tepid water and arrowroot. Bring to a boil over a medium heat. Partially cover the saucepan and reduce the heat to low. Simmer for 1 hour.

♦ In a small bowl, combine the arrowroot and tepid water. Stir well. Stir the mixture into the soup and turn the heat up to medium. Continue stirring until the soup begins to bubble. Reduce the heat to low. Simmer the soup, uncovered, for 2 minutes. Pour the soup into a glass bowl and chill for 1 hour. Serve cold.

Beef Goulash

SERVES 8

There is perhaps no dish so readily identifable with Hungary than goulash. There are at least 80 standard variations calling for a variety of different ingredients. Below is a traditional beef goulash recipe.

4 pounds lean beef sirloin, cut into small pieces

5 tablespoons margarine

1 large onion, coarsely chopped

1 medium-sized green pepper, seeded and finely diced

3 cups beef broth

2 tablespoons flour

1 large tomato, peeled, seeded and coarsely chopped

3 tablespoons poppy seeds

2 tablespoons Hungarian sweet paprika

$\frac{1}{4}$ cup dry red wine

1 pound egg noodles

Melt the margarine in a large saucepan over a low heat. Add the onion, tomato and green pepper and sauté for 5 minutes.
♦ Add the beef, paprika, red wine, beef broth, flour and poppy seeds. Simmer for 30 minutes. Add 1 cup water, cover, and simmer for 90 minutes.
♦ While the goulash simmers, cook the egg noodles in a large pan of boiling water. Drain well. Serve the goulash on a bed of noodles.

Asparagus with Nutmeg

SERVES 8

The addition of nutmeg to this simple asparagus dish gives it a surprising flavor.

$\frac{1}{2}$ cup margarine

2 garlic cloves, quartered

1 teaspoon grated nutmeg

1 tablespoon finely chopped onion

2 pounds fresh asparagus, trimmed

Preheat the oven to 375°F. In a small saucepan, melt the margarine over a low heat. Add the garlic, nutmeg and onion.
♦ Place the asparagus in a large baking dish. Pour the margarine mixture over the asparagus and bake for 18 minutes. Serve hot.

New Potatoes with Wine

SERVES 6—8

New potatoes are delicious served this way. If medium-hot paprika is not available, use sweet paprika and add $\frac{1}{4}$ teaspoon cayenne pepper.

$2\frac{1}{2}$ pounds new potatoes, quartered

2 cups white wine

1 garlic clove, halved

1 teaspoon medium-hot Hungarian paprika

Cook the new potatoes in a large pot of boiling water until tender, about 25 to 30 minutes.
♦ Drain the potatoes well and return them to the saucepan. Add the wine, garlic and paprika. Simmer over a low heat for 20 minutes. Serve hot.

Walnut Apricot Pancakes

SERVES 8

Quite similar to French crêpes, this traditional Hungarian dessert will satisfy any sweet tooth.

4 eggs

$1\frac{1}{4}$ cups water

$\frac{1}{2}$ cup soda water

2 cups sifted flour

6 tablespoons sugar

$\frac{1}{2}$ teaspoon salt

2 teaspoons pure vanilla extract

1 cup apricot preserves

$\frac{1}{4}$ cup strawberry preserves

1 cup finely chopped walnuts

8 tablespoons margarine

$\frac{1}{4}$ cup superfine brown sugar

In a medium-sized mixing bowl beat the eggs. Add the soda water, salt and vanilla extract. Mix well. Fold in the flour and sugar. Stir until the batter has an even consistency.
♦ Combine the apricot preserves, strawberry preserves and chopped walnuts in a bowl. Mix well.
♦ For each pancake, melt 1 teaspoon of the margarine in a small skillet over a medium heat. Pour a thin layer of batter into the skillet. Cook the pancake for 2—3 minutes. Turn the pancake and cook for 1 minute.
♦ Fill each pancake with 3 teaspoons of the preserves and nut mixture. Roll each pancake into a cylinder and place it in a baking dish in a slow oven to keep warm. Sprinkle each pancake with brown sugar before serving. Serve warm.

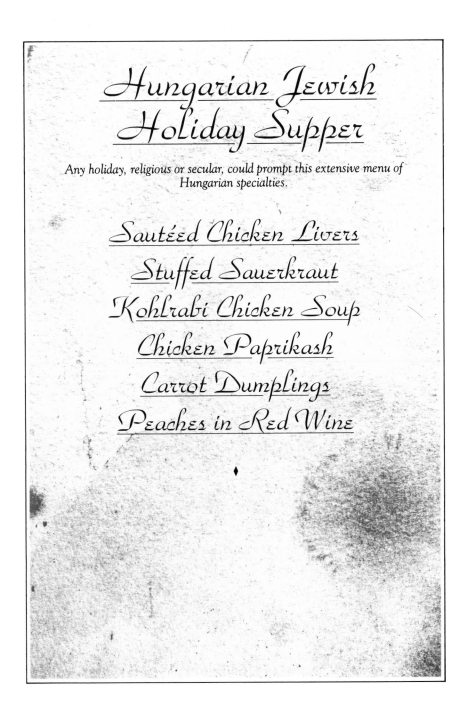

Hungarian Jewish Holiday Supper

Any holiday, religious or secular, could prompt this extensive menu of Hungarian specialties.

Sautéed Chicken Livers

Stuffed Sauerkraut

Kohlrabi Chicken Soup

Chicken Paprikash

Carrot Dumplings

Peaches in Red Wine

♦

Sautéed Chicken Livers

SERVES 8

Featuring two different kinds of wine, this recipe has a decidedly Continental flavor.

$\frac{1}{4}$ cup chicken fat

$1\frac{1}{2}$ pounds fresh chicken livers

1 cup white wine

$\frac{1}{4}$ cup dry sherry

1 tablespoon chopped parsley

1 tablespoon finely chopped onion

1 garlic clove, finely chopped

1 small shallot, finely chopped

$\frac{1}{4}$ teaspoon salt

$\frac{1}{4}$ teaspoon ground white pepper

Melt the chicken fat in a large skillet over a low heat. Add the chicken livers and sauté until browned, about 5 minutes. Add the remaining ingredients, raise the heat to medium, cover and cook for 5 minutes.

♦ Remove the cover and cook until the liquid is almost gone, stirring occasionally. Serve with crackers or crusty bread.

Stuffed Sauerkraut

SERVES 8

This is the Hungarian version of stuffed cabbage. It is unique in that the sauce is neither red nor sweet.

10 large white cabbage leaves

$\frac{1}{4}$ cup chicken fat

2 pounds ground veal

1 cup cooked rice

3 garlic cloves, quartered

1 cup finely chopped onion

$\frac{1}{4}$ teaspoon salt

$\frac{1}{4}$ teaspoon white pepper

1 teaspoon Hungarian sweet paprika

Cook the cabbage leaves in a large pot of boiling water for 5 to 8 minutes or until they are soft. Drain well and set aside.

♦ In a large saucepan, melt the chicken fat. Add the ground veal, rice, garlic, onions, salt and pepper. Cook over a low heat, stirring often, until the veal loses its raw look. Cover and simmer for 20 minutes, stirring frequently.

♦ Add the sauerkraut and paprika to the veal mixture and cook, stirring frequently, for 2 minutes.

♦ Spoon 3 tablespoons of the veal mixture on to the center of each cabbage leaf. Roll up the cabbage leaves, tucking in the edges of the leaves as you roll.

♦ Place the cabbage rolls in a large saucepan. Add 1 cup of cold water and cover. Simmer over a low heat for 50 minutes. Serve warm.

Kohlrabi Chicken Soup

SERVES 8

No cuisine makes more use of kohlrabi, a rather obscure root vegetable, than the Hungarian. Fresh kohlrabi can be purchased at most well-stocked markets.

3 pound chicken, cut into pieces

3 medium onions, halved

8 cups chicken broth

1 leek

½ teaspoon salt

¼ teaspoon black pepper

3 cups fresh kohlrabi, peeled and cut into small pieces

½ cup coarsely chopped fresh parsley

3 tablespoons margarine

¼ cup white wine

Place the chicken, onions, chicken broth, leek, salt and pepper in a large soup pot. Simmer, covered, over a medium heat for 50 minutes. Add the kohlrabi, parsley, margarine and wine. Simmer, covered, for an additional 35 minutes.
♦ Remove the chicken and use it in another dish. Serve the soup hot.

Chicken Paprikash

SERVES 6—8

This delectable chicken dish is the perfect centerpiece for a Hungarian holiday dinner. Although most cook books suggest serving it with egg noodles, for true authenticity it should be served on a bed of rice.

4 pound chicken, cut into pieces

½ pound margarine

1 cup shredded carrots

½ cup chopped onions

3 garlic cloves, quartered

½ cup flour

4 teaspoons Hungarian sweet paprika

¼ teaspoon salt

¼ teaspoon black pepper

½ cup red wine

4 cups chicken broth

Place all the ingredients except for 2 cups of the chicken broth in a large soup pot. Simmer, covered, over a low heat for 1 hour.
♦ Add the remaining chicken broth, reduce the heat to very low and simmer, covered, for 1 hour longer. Serve on a bed or rice.

Carrot Dumplings

SERVES 6—8

In the days when refined white sugar was scarce and expensive, sweet dishes were often made with naturally sweet carrots. These carrot dumplings are both sweet and hearty.

10 large carrots, peeled and finely shredded

1 large sweet potato, cooked, peeled and mashed

4 tablespoons chicken fat

$\frac{1}{2}$ cup potato flour

$\frac{1}{4}$ teaspoon salt

1 cup water

8 tablespoons margarine

1 large onion, finely diced

Cook the carrots in a saucepan of boiling water until tender, about 8 to 10 minutes. Drain well.

♦ Combine the carrots and mashed sweet potato in a large mixing bowl. Mash together until the consistency is even. Shape the mixture into thick, round cakes.

♦ Melt the chicken fat in a large skillet. Add the potato flour and brown it. Add the carrot dumpling cakes and water. Cover the skillet and lower the heat. Steam the dumplings for 3 to 5 minutes. Remove the dumplings from the skillet and drain them on paper towels.

♦ In a small saucepan, melt the margarine. Add the onion and salt. Simmer for 5 minutes over a very low heat.

♦ Pour the margarine mixture over the carrot dumplings before serving.

Peaches in Red Wine

SERVES 6—8

This dish makes a refreshing end to a substantial meal.

2 cups red wine

1 tablespoon currant preserves

1 tablespoon sugar

$1\frac{1}{2}$ pounds canned peaches, drained

In a medium-sized mixing bowl, combine the wine, preserves and sugar. Stir with a fork until the consistency is even and any lumps are dissolved. Add the peaches. Chill for at least 1 hour before serving.

Romanian Jewish Dinner

This menu is a sampling of traditional Romanian cuisine. Some dishes, such as the nearly flourless walnut torte, are Jewish in origin. Others, like mamaliga, are classic Romanian dishes enjoyed by Jews and Gentiles alike.

Sour Soup

Mamaliga

Stuffed Beef Hearts

Walnut Torte

◆

Sour Soup

SERVES 8

Found only in Romania, this unusual soup gets its savory flavor from the veal.

1 tablespoons olive oil

1 large carrot, finely chopped

$\frac{1}{4}$ cup chopped celery

2 onions, diced

$1\frac{1}{2}$ cups water

$\frac{1}{4}$ cup chopped parsley

4 cups sauerkraut juice

2 beaten eggs

2 slices bread, soaked in water and drained

$\frac{1}{2}$ teaspoon salt

$\frac{1}{4}$ teaspoon black pepper

$\frac{1}{4}$ cup cooked rice

$\frac{1}{2}$ teaspoon chopped fresh dill

$1\frac{1}{2}$ pounds ground veal

Heat the olive oil in a large saucepan over a medium heat. Add the carrots, celery and onions and sauté for 8 minutes, stirring frequently. Add the water and parsley to the saucepan and bring to a boil. Cook for 1 minute. Add the sauerkraut juice and reduce the heat slightly. Cook for 15 minutes.

♦ In a large mixing bowl, combine the eggs, bread, salt, pepper, rice, dill and veal. Mix with a fork until the consistency is even. Form the veal mixture into balls approximately 1 inch in diameter. Drop the meatballs into the simmering soup and reduce the heat to low. Simmer for 40 minutes and serve.

Mamaliga

SERVES 6—8

Mamaliga is a staple food in Romania.

$1\frac{1}{4}$ cups yellow corn meal

$1\frac{1}{2}$ tablespoons chicken fat

2 cups boiling water

$\frac{1}{2}$ teaspoon salt

$\frac{1}{4}$ teaspoon black pepper

2 eggs, separated

$1\frac{3}{4}$ cups buttermilk

$1\frac{1}{4}$ teaspoons baking soda

4 tablespoons melted margarine

In a large pot, combine the corn meal with the chicken fat and boiling water. Mix until the consistency of the dough is even. Add the salt, pepper, egg yolks, buttermilk and baking soda. Combine thoroughly.

♦ Beat the egg whites until they are stiff. Fold them into the corn meal mixture.

♦ Grease a large casserole dish with 1 tablespoon of the melted margarine. Preheat the oven to 325°F. Scrape the corn meal mixture into the casserole with a spatula. Bake for 1 hour 15 minutes. Pour the remaining melted margarine over the mamaliga before serving.

Stuffed Beef Hearts

SERVES 8

The Romanian Jews perfected the difficult art of preparing variety meats, as this dish illustrates.

2 beef hearts, prepared for stuffing

4 tablespoons olive oil

3 garlic cloves, finely chopped

4 tablespoons chopped fresh parsley

$\frac{1}{2}$ cup diced mushrooms

$\frac{1}{2}$ cup golden seedless raisins

$\frac{1}{2}$ cup dried apricots

2 hard-boiled eggs, finely chopped

$\frac{1}{2}$ cup vegetable oil

3 cups tomato sauce

2 tablespoons tomato paste

Coat the beef hearts inside and out with the olive oil. In a large mixing bowl, combine the garlic, parsley, mushrooms, raisins, apricots and eggs thoroughly.
♦ Stuff the beef hearts with the mixture. Tie the hearts closed with kitchen twine.
♦ Heat the vegetable oil in a large saucepan over a medium heat. Add the beef hearts and brown on all sides. Add the tomato sauce and tomato paste. Cover and simmer for 90 minutes over a low heat. Split the hearts in half and serve.

Walnut Torte

SERVES 8

An ingenious invention of the Romanian Jews, imitating their Viennese relatives.

1 pound shelled walnut halves

5 tablespoons unsalted margarine

$\frac{1}{2}$ tablespoon flour

5 eggs, at room temperature, separated

$\frac{1}{2}$ cup sugar

1 teaspoon pure vanilla extract

$\frac{3}{4}$ cup peach preserves

1 tablespoon instant cocoa

4 ounces semi-sweet chocolate, crumbled

1 tablespoon boiling water

Preheat the oven to 350°F. Spread the walnuts in a single layer in a large baking pan and roast them for 12 to 15 minutes. Chop the walnuts finely.
♦ Grease a 9 × 3 inch baking dish with $\frac{1}{2}$ tablespoon margarine. Dust the pan with the flour.
♦ In a large mixing bowl, gradually combine the egg yolks with the sugar, beating constantly until the egg yolks are lemon-colored. Stir in the vanilla extract.
♦ In another bowl, beat the egg whites until they are stiff. Gradually beat the walnuts into the egg whites. Gently fold the egg whites into the egg yolk mixture. Scrape the batter into the greased baking dish. Bake for 25 minutes.
♦ Invert the baking dish over a cooling rack, remove the dish, and leave to cool.
♦ Heat the peach preserves until they are warm. Spread them on the cake.
♦ Melt the cocoa and chocolate over a low heat, gradually adding the margarine.
♦ Spread the chocolate icing over the cake. Chill for 1 hour before serving.

Yugoslav Jewish Supper

Although the cuisines of Yugoslavia and Czechoslovakia are hearty and pleasing, they do not have a large repertoire of desserts. Most meals end with fresh fruit in season, a plain cake or perhaps some home-made preserves. This simple four-course supper is guaranteed to fill the hungriest stomach.

Vegetable Caviar
Eggplant Soup
Yugoslavian Leg of Lamb
Serbian Apple Cake
Fresh Fruit

◆

Vegetable Caviar

SERVES 6—8

Serve this delectable vegetarian dish in exactly the same way as real caviar — by itself, accompanied by thin slices of dark bread and perhaps a squeeze of lemon.

1 small eggplant, peeled

1 small acorn squash, halved and seeded

3 large green peppers, seeded

½ teaspoon salt

½ teaspoon black pepper

½ teaspoon finely chopped garlic

3 tablespoons lemon juice

6 tablespoons vegetable oil

3 tablespoons finely chopped fresh parsley

Preheat the oven to 475°F. Place the eggplant, acorn squash, and green peppers in a baking dish. Bake for 30 minutes and remove the peppers. Bake the acorn squash and eggplant for 15 minutes longer.

♦ Cut the peppers into strips. Cut the eggplant into cubes. Scoop the pulp from the squash and discard the skin.

♦ Combine the eggplant, peppers and squash in a medium-sized mixing bowl. Chop and mix thoroughly until the mixture is well combined. Add the salt, black pepper, garlic, lemon juice, vegetable oil and parsley. Blend thoroughly. Chill for at least 2 hours before serving.

Eggplant Soup

SERVES 6—8

This unusual soup shows a touch of Turkish influence.

½ cup olive oil

1 cup mushrooms, quartered

1 large onion, coarsely chopped

1 large tomato, cut into eighths

1 large eggplant, peeled and diced

3 cups beef broth

½ teaspoon dried parsley

¼ teaspoon salt

¼ teaspoon white pepper

¼ teaspoon dried thyme

¼ teaspoon dried marjoram

¼ teaspoon grated nutmeg

Heat the olive oil in a large pot over a low heat. Add the mushrooms, onion and tomato and sauté for 10 minutes.

♦ Add the remaining ingredients to the pot. Cover and simmer for 35 to 40 minutes. Serve hot.

Yugoslavian Leg of Lamb

SERVES 6—8

Use the best leg of lamb you can find for this traditional Passover dish.

7-8 pound leg of lamb, boned and tied
1 teaspoon salt
1 cup red wine vinegar
3 bay leaves
2 cups water
$2\frac{1}{2}$ cups diced onions
$\frac{1}{4}$ cup coarsely chopped fresh parsley
$\frac{1}{2}$ teaspoon dried thyme
$\frac{1}{2}$ teaspoon black pepper
4 large tomatoes, coarsely chopped
2 tablespoons chicken fat

Rub the leg of lamb with the salt. Put the lamb in a large casserole.
♦ In a small saucepan combine the bay leaves, vinegar, water, onions, parsley, thyme, pepper and tomatoes. Bring the liquid to a boil over a high heat. Cook for 1 minute and remove the saucepan from the heat. Cool the mixture to room temperature and pour it over the lamb. Leave the lamb to marinate in the refrigerator for 6 hours, uncovered. Turn the lamb every $1\frac{1}{2}$ hours.
♦ Preheat the oven to 375°F. Melt the chicken fat in a small saucepan over a medium heat. Remove the lamb from the refrigerator. Pour the chicken fat over the lamb. Roast the lamb for 2 hours, basting every 30 minutes. If the liquid in the casserole starts to boil too fast, reduce the heat to 350°F. Save the pan drippings for gravy.

Serbian Apple Cake

SERVES 6—8

In the days of the Austro-Hungarian empire, Yugoslavia was called Serbia.

$\frac{2}{3}$ cup margarine
1 cup sugar
2 eggs, separated
2 tablespoons fresh lemon juice
2 cups flour
2 tablespoons ground almonds
2 teaspoons baking powder
$\frac{1}{2}$ teaspoon salt
$\frac{1}{4}$ teaspoon grated nutmeg
4 apples, peeled, cored and thinly sliced

Preheat the oven to 350°F. Beat the margarine until creamy. Add $\frac{3}{4}$ cup of the sugar and continue beating until the mixture is fluffy. Beat in the egg yolks, one at a time. Beat in the lemon juice.
♦ In another mixing bowl, beat the egg whites until they are stiff.
♦ In another bowl sift together the flour, almonds, baking powder, salt and nutmeg.
♦ Alternately add the egg white and flour mixtures to the margarine, beating after each addition. Pour the batter into a 9 inch deep cake pan with spring clip. Press the apple slices into the top of the batter. Sprinkle the cake with the rest of the sugar and bake for 50 minutes. Allow the cake to cool for 10 minutes before serving.

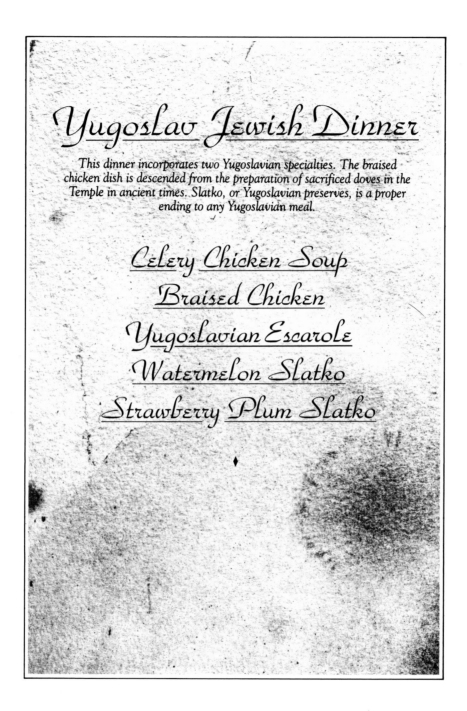

Yugoslav Jewish Dinner

This dinner incorporates two Yugoslavian specialties. The braised chicken dish is descended from the preparation of sacrificed doves in the Temple in ancient times. Slatko, or Yugoslavian preserves, is a proper ending to any Yugoslavian meal.

Celery Chicken Soup
Braised Chicken
Yugoslavian Escarole
Watermelon Slatko
Strawberry Plum Slatko

Celery Chicken Soup

SERVES 6—8

This Balkan variation on chicken soup used celeriac for its distinct flavor.

6 cups chicken broth
2 large celeriac, peeled and sliced
$\frac{1}{2}$ cup coarsely chopped celery
$\frac{1}{2}$ cup chopped leeks
1 small endive, chopped
2 large carrots, diced
$\frac{1}{2}$ teaspoon salt
$\frac{1}{2}$ teaspoon white pepper

In a large soup pot, bring the chicken broth to a boil. Add the remaining ingredients, reduce the heat to low and simmer for 40 minutes. Serve hot.

Braised Chicken

SERVES 6—8

This dish is traditionally made with squab or game birds. Small chickens or Cornish game hens can be used instead.

3 small chickens, split
6 tablespoons olive oil
4 tablespoons margarine
2 garlic cloves, quartered
2 onions, coarsely chopped
2 cups mushrooms, quartered
2 tablespoons lemon juice
2 cups white wine
2 tablespoons chopped parsley
$\frac{1}{2}$ teaspoon dried sage
$\frac{1}{4}$ teaspoon dried marjoram
$\frac{1}{2}$ teaspoon salt
$\frac{1}{2}$ teaspoon black pepper

Put the chickens, skin-side up, into a very large saucepan or 2 smaller ones. Pour the olive oil over the chickens.

♦ In a small saucepan, melt the margarine. Add the garlic, onions and mushrooms. Sauté over a low heat for 3 to 5 minutes. Add the lemon juice, wine, parsley, sage, marjoram, salt and pepper and stir well. Pour the mixture evenly over the chickens. Cover and simmer over a medium heat for 15 minutes. Reduce the heat to low and simmer for 45 minutes or until the chickens are tender. Add more wine during the cooking if needed.

Yugoslavian Escarole

SERVES 6—8

The escarole that we enjoy in salads can also be served as a delicious hot vegetable.

1 large head curly escarole, trimmed and coarsely chopped
1 large tomato, cut into eighths
4 garlic cloves, halved
1 small onion, finely chopped
$\frac{1}{2}$ teaspoon salt
$\frac{1}{2}$ teaspoon black pepper
2 cups water
4 tablespoons olive oil

Place all the ingredients into a medium-sized saucepan. Cover the saucepan and simmer over a medium heat for 15 minutes. Reduce the heat to low and simmer for 20 minutes longer. Serve hot.

Watermelon Slatko

MAKES 3 PINTS

Watermelon preserve should be served with Strawberry Plum Slatko in silver dishes.

2 pounds watermelon rind, all pink flesh removed
1 teaspoon pure vanilla extract
4 tablespoons lemon juice
2 pounds sugar

With a sharp knife, remove the green outer skin from the watermelon rind. Cut the rind into small cubes. Place the watermelon rind cubes into a 3 quart saucepan. Add enough water to cover the rind cubes and bring the liquid to a boil. Cook for 1 minute and drain. Repeat the process with fresh water. Cover the rinds with water a third time and simmer over a low heat for 20 minutes. Drain well.
◆ Add $\frac{3}{4}$ cup water to the rind along with the vanilla extract and the lemon juice. Raise the heat to medium and gradually stir in the sugar. When all the sugar has dissolved, reduce the heat to low and simmer for 2 hours.
◆ Store in sterilized glass hars in the refrigerator.

Strawberry Plum Slatko

MAKES 2 PINTS

Serve slatko with plain cakes or simple sugar cookies.

2 cups sugar
$\frac{3}{4}$ pound damsons or other ripe purple plums, pitted and quartered
$\frac{1}{2}$ pound fresh strawberries, quartered
3 tablespoons lemon juice

Combine the sugar, plums and strawberries in a large saucepan. Stir well. Cover and cook over a medium heat for 10 minutes. Stir with a fork to make sure the sugar melts. Cook for a further 20 minutes or until the sugar is completely dissolved.
◆ Add the lemon juice and cook for 10 minutes longer. Remove the saucepan from the heat and leave the slatko to stand, covered, at room temperature for 12 hours.
◆ Store in sterilized glass jars in the refrigerator.

Mamaliga ABOVE LEFT (OPPOSITE) is a staple food in
Romania (page 110).

◆

Eggplant Soup ABOVE RIGHT (OPPOSITE) comes from
Yugoslavia. (page 113).

◆

Yugoslavian Escarole BELOW (OPPOSITE) goes well
with Braised Chicken (page 117).

◆

Slatko ABOVE is a traditional end to a Yugoslavian
meal (page 117).

Germany and Austria

The Jews have been part of the German-speaking world for the last thousand years. In the fourth century, Cologne had a large Jewish population. By the eleventh century, Jews were an integral part of the Germanic cultural and economic world. It was in Germany in the 1850s that the *Haskalah* or enlightenment movement began, which paved the way for the assimilation of German Jews. Three of the greatest thinkers of the late nineteenth and early twentieth century, Karl Marx, Sigmund Freud and Albert Einstein, were Jews. By the beginning of the twentieth century, Jews in Germany and Austria had become an influential force in general culture.

Nevertheless, the German-speaking Jews were always subject to fierce anti-Semitism. The culmination of this anti-Semitism came with the Holocaust of World War II. The Jewish population of Germany, over half a million before the war, was virtually destroyed. Today, about 30,000 Jews continue to live in Germany.

Jews have lived in Austria, and in particular Vienna, since Roman times. The first ghetto there was instituted in the thirteenth century, situated around the square today called *Judenplatz*. In the thirteenth and fourteenth centuries the Viennese Jewish community was recognized as one of the most important in Europe. Persecution in the fifteenth century led to a sharp drop in their numbers. The Jews returned slowly after 1675 and gradually became prominent again. In 1781 the Emperor Joseph II granted increased liberties to the Jews, anticipating the emancipation that came in the nineteenth century. In 1826 the *Stadttempel*, the main synagogue in Vienna and the only currently active one, was dedicated. At the end of the nineteenth century and during the first quarter of this century, Vienna was a center of Zionism. Dr Theodore Herzl, the guiding force behind Zionism, lived and worked in Vienna. The Viennese Jews accomplished remarkable things during the golden age from 1848 to 1938. This thriving community of 180,000 was annihilated between 1939 and 1945, and the current population is about 10,000.

As the Jews became more and more integrated into the fabric of German life, so did their cooking. They were fond of sausages and wursts, and took their sauerbraten seriously. Herring salads were popular, as were compôtes for dessert. German-Jewish baking was said to be lighter than that of the Gentiles because no lard was used in the dough.

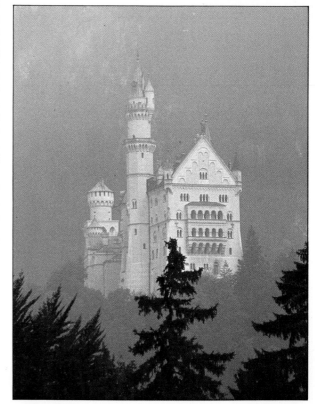

Some of the most famous Jewish dishes come from Germany and Austria. Sadly the recipes have been preserved only by those who fled persecution.

Challah ABOVE *is traditionally eaten on the
Sabbath. Its origins are very ancient (page 126).*

◆

Green Beans Paprika BELOW *is a staple dish of
Austrian Jewish cooking (page 131).*

German Austrian Friday Night Dinner

This Friday night repast features a traditional roast stuffed chicken, a delicious German variation on stuffed cabbage, and a delicate purée of mixed vegetables, a German speciality.

Challah
Bean, Mushroom and Asparagus Purée
Traditional Roast Chicken
German Austrian Stuffed Cabbage
Sponge Cake with Brandy Sauce

Challah

MAKES 2 LOAVES

The origins of Challah, the twisted egg bread traditionally eaten on the Sabbath and holidays, are very ancient. In the days of the Temple, women would offer a portion of their bread dough, called the Challah, to the priests as a dedication to God. Challah recipes always make two loaves, and both loaves are traditionally placed on the table on Friday night. This is in commemoration of the double portion of manna the Israelites received on Friday as they wandered in the desert after fleeing Egypt.

1 cup lukewarm water
3 packages active dry yeast
5 teaspoons sugar
6 cups flour
1½ teaspoons salt
3 eggs
¼ cup vegetable oil
1 egg yolk

In a small bowl combine the water, yeast and 1 teaspoon sugar. Leave it to stand for 3 minutes and then stir until the yeast is dissolved. Leave it for a further 5 minutes.
♦ Combine 4 cups of the flour with the salt and remaining sugar in a large, deep mixing bowl. Make a well in the center of the flour and pour in the yeast mixture. Add the eggs and vegetable oil. Gently stir until the ingredients are blended together. Stirring more vigorously, blend in the remaining flour.
♦ Turn the dough out onto a lightly floured surface and knead for 20 minutes with a rolling pin, flattening the dough with the rolling pin, gathering it back into a ball and flattening again. Place the dough ball into a bowl, cover with a clean cloth, and leave it to stand for 45 minutes or until it is nearly doubled in bulk.
♦ Turn the dough out and knead for 5 minutes. Leave to rest for 5 minutes.
♦ Cut the dough in half with a sharp knife. Cut each half into thirds. Roll each piece of dough into a cylinder that tapers at each end. Pinch the ends of the 3 dough cylinders together. Braid the cylinders and pinch the other ends together. Repeat with the remaining dough. Place the challahs on a lightly greased baking sheet and leave them to stand for 30 minutes.
♦ Preheat the oven to 400°F. In a small bowl, beat the egg yolk with 2 tablespoons cold water. Brush the tops of the challahs with the egg yolk and bake for 20 minutes. Reduce the oven temperature to 375°F and bake for 40 minutes longer, or until the challahs are lightly browned. Cool on a rack.

Bean, Mushroom and Asparagus Purée

SERVES 6

This dish is adapted to kosher requirements from the haute gentile cuisine of Germany.

1 pound fresh green beans
½ pound mushrooms
1 pound fresh asparagus
1 tablespoon clarified margarine
½ teaspoon nutmeg
½ teaspoon white pepper
½ teaspoon salt
1 egg yolk

Fill a large pot to the depth of 1½ inches with cold water. Add the green beans, mushrooms and asparagus. Cook over a low heat for 5 minute. Add the clarified margarine, nutmeg, pepper and salt. Cook for a further 1 minutes.

♦ Place the vegetables, along with the egg yolk and ½ cup of the cooking liquid, in a blender or food processor. Purée in bursts of 30 seconds until the vegetable mixture is smooth and well blended. Serve hot with croûtons.

Traditional Roast Chicken

SERVES 6

The hallmark of a German-Jewish Sabbath meal, this traditional dish is still a big favorite today.

3½-4 pound roasting chicken, with liver
1 teaspoon salt
1 tablespoon ground ginger
2 garlic cloves, finely chopped
1 teaspoon cayenne pepper
2 cups unflavored breadcrumbs
½ cup chopped celery
½ cup chopped mushrooms
¼ cup shredded carrots
2 tablespoons vegetable oil
1 tablespoon chopped fresh parsley or 1 teaspoon dried parsley
½ teaspoon dried thyme
½ teaspoon dried marjoram
4 tablespoons melted margarine
1 cup boiling water
3 pounds potatoes, cut into sixths
3 large onions, cut into sixths

Preheat the oven to 350°F. Place the cleaned chicken on a greased roasting pan. Reserve the chicken liver. Sprinkle the skin with ½ teaspoon each of the salt, garlic, ginger and cayenne pepper. Roast the chicken for 30 minutes.

♦ While the chicken roasts, prepare the stuffing. In a mixing bowl combine the breadcrumbs with the celery, mushrooms, carrots, oil, and the remaining salt, garlic, ginger and cayenne pepper. Add the parsley, thyme and marjoram. Mix well.

♦ Put the chicken liver in a small saucepan and add enough cold water to cover. Bring to the boil and cook until the liver is done, about 10 minutes. Drain well. Chop the liver coarsely. Add the chopped liver to the stuffing mixture. Add the melted margarine and the boiling water. Mix well.

♦ Remove the chicken from the oven and fill the cavity with the stuffing. Arrange the potato and onion pieces around the chicken in the roasting pan. Return the chicken to the oven and roast for 1½ to 2 hours basting with the pan drippings every 30 minutes. Sprinkle the chicken, potatoes and onions with paprika after the final basting.

German Austrian Stuffed Cabbage

SERVES 6 TO 8

> 1 medium-sized green cabbage, cored
>
> 4 tablespoons vegetable oil
>
> 2 large onions, chopped
>
> 2 cups cooked rice
>
> 4 eggs, beaten
>
> $\frac{1}{4}$ cup golden seedless raisins
>
> $\frac{1}{2}$ teaspoon salt
>
> 1 teaspoon black pepper
>
> 2 tablespoons margarine
>
> $\frac{1}{2}$ cup seedless white grapes, halved
>
> $\frac{1}{2}$ cup shredded red cabbage
>
> 6 canned tomatoes, chopped

Separate the leaves from the cabbage. Blanch the leaves in a large pot of boiling water for 5 minutes. Drain well.

◆ Heat the oil in a skillet. Add the onions and brown over a low heat. Add the rice, eggs and raisins. Cook, stirring frequently, for 30 seconds. Add the salt, pepper, margarine and grapes. Cook, stirring frequently, for 90 seconds.

◆ Place 2 to 3 tablespoons of the rice filling at the edge of a cabbage leaf. Roll the leaf up, tucking the ends under. Repeat with the remaining cabbage leaves until the rice filling is used up. Coarsely chop the remaining cabbage leaves.

◆ Heat the remaining oil in a large skillet over a moderate heat. Add the chopped green cabbage and the red cabbage. Sauté for 3 to 4 minutes. Add the stuffed cabbage leaves and tomatoes. Cover and cook for 12 minutes.

Sponge Cake with Brandy Sauce

MAKES 1 CAKE

Sponge cake is a traditional dessert served on the Sabbath and holidays.

> 8 eggs, separated
>
> 2 cups sugar
>
> $2\frac{1}{2}$ cups sifted flour
>
> $\frac{1}{2}$ teaspoon cream of tartar
>
> 3 teaspoons pure vanilla extract
>
> $\frac{1}{2}$ cup brandy
>
> $\frac{1}{2}$ cup fresh or drained canned cherries, pitted
>
> $\frac{1}{2}$ cup drained canned mandarin oranges
>
> $\frac{1}{2}$ cup orange juice

Preheat the oven to 300°F. In a large bowl, beat the egg whites until they are stiff but not dry. Beat in $1\frac{1}{2}$ cups of the sugar.

◆ In another bowl, beat the egg yolks with the remaining sugar. Add the egg yolks to the egg whites. Fold in the flour, cream of tartar, 2 teaspoons of the vanilla extract and $\frac{1}{4}$ cup of the brandy.

◆ Pour the batter into a greased 9 inch square baking pan. Bake for 70 minutes. Cool the cake in the pan.

◆ To make the brandy sauce, combine the remaining vanilla extract and brandy with the cherries, mandarin oranges and orange juice in a bowl. Mix well. Spoon the sauce over slices of the cake just before serving.

German Austrian Dairy Lunch

This elegant lunch begins with a savory onion pudding. It features poached sole and the famous Viennese strudel. The green beans with paprika are a reminder of Vienna's history as a crossroads between eastern and western Europe.

Onion Pudding
Egg Salad
Poached Sole
Green Beans Paprika
Viennese Strudel

Onion Pudding

SERVES 6

A savory treat and an unusual beginning for a classic German-Jewish luncheon, onion puddings were very popular among the Viennese Jews who invented the dish. Onion puddings also became standard in Polish-Jewish cooking.

4 tablespoons butter

$\frac{1}{4}$ cup white wine

$\frac{1}{2}$ teaspoon dried dill

2 garlic cloves, quartered

6 large onions, coarsely chopped

3 tablespoons sugar

$1\frac{1}{2}$ cups unflavored breadcrumbs

1 cup crumbled matzoh

1 cup diced mild cheese

Melt 3 tablespoons of the butter in a large saucepan and add the wine, dill and garlic. Reduce the heat to low and add the onions and sugar. Stir gently until the sugar has completely dissolved. Simmer for another 5 minutes. Remove the saucepan from the heat.

♦ Preheat the oven to 375°F. Grease a 9 inch pie dish with the remaining butter. Spoon a thin layer of the onion mixture into the dish. Cover with a thin layer of the breadcrumbs and crumbled matzoh. Repeat the process until the onion, breadcrumbs and matzoh are used up.

♦ Top the pudding with the cheese and bake for 15 minutes, or until the cheese is melted and lightly browned. Remove the pudding from the oven, cut it into squares or wedges and serve hot.

Egg Salad

SERVES 6

This piquant version of egg salad is served as an appetizer, not as a sandwich filling.

6 hard-boiled eggs

4 tablespoons mayonnaise

1 carrot, diced

1 large celery stalk, diced

1 small onion, finely chopped

2 tablespoons chopped green pepper

1 large pimento, chopped

2 tablespoons sweet pickle relish

1 tablespoon Dijon-style mustard

$\frac{1}{2}$ teaspoon celery salt

1 teaspoon Worcestershire sauce

1 teaspoon cayenne pepper

1 teaspoon paprika

In a large mixing bowl, combine all the ingredients except the paprika. Mix roughly with a fork until the consistency, texture and colour of the mixture is even throughout.

♦ Arrange the egg salad on a bed of lettuce. Sprinkle with paprika. Chill for 10 minutes before serving.

Poached Sole

SERVES 6

This method for poaching fresh fish was extremely popular among affluent German-Jewish families in the nineteenth century.

2 cups dry vermouth

2 large onions, sliced

4 parsley sprigs

1 bay leaf

2 tablespoons fresh basil leaves or 1 teaspoon dried basil

1 tablespoon black pepper

1 cup chopped celery

1 quart water

$\frac{1}{2}$ teaspoon dried thyme

4 pounds sole or flounder fillets

6 tomatoes

4 egg yolks, beaten

1 cup heavy cream

To make the poaching liquid, combine the vermouth, onions, parsley, bay leaf, basil, black pepper, celery, water, thyme and salt in a large pot. Simmer over a low heat for 30 minutes.

♦ Arrange the fillets on a large square of cheesecloth. Top with the tomatoes and wrap with the cheesecloth.

♦ Strain the broth into a fish poacher or large skillet. Add the wrapped fish and tomatoes. Cover and simmer gently over a low heat for 10 minutes.

♦ Remove the fish and tomatoes from the poacher. Remove the cheesecloth and arrange the fillets on a warm serving platter. Keep warm while you make the sauce.

♦ Whisk the egg yolks and cream into the remaining broth in the poacher. Cook over a medium heat, stirring constantly, for 5 minutes or until the sauce thickens. Do not let boil. Pour the sauce over the fish and serve with lemon slices.

Green Beans Paprika

SERVES 6

This dish is a staple of Austrian-Jewish cooking with strong Hungarian influence.

2 pounds fresh green beans, trimmed and halved

8 tablespoons butter

2 cups coarsely chopped scallions

1 tablespoon flour

2 cups soured cream

1 tablespoon sweet paprika

$\frac{1}{2}$ teaspoon salt

Cook the green beans in a large pot of boiling water until they are tender but still crisp, about 7 minutes. Drain well.

♦ Melt the butter in a medium-sized saucepan over a low heat. Add the scallions and cook, stirring frequently, for 4 to 5 minutes, or until they are translucent. Remove the saucepan from the heat and stir in the paprika. Set aside.

♦ Combine the flour and soured cream in a small bowl until they are well mixed. Add the mixture to the scallions. Add the salt. Simmer the mixture over a low heat for 5 minutes. Add the beans and simmer for 5 minutes longer. Serve hot.

Viennese Strudel

SERVES 8

The acknowledged champions of the baking world, the Viennese are proud of their strudel. Strudel dough should be so thin that newsprint can be read through it. Prepared strudel dough is now widely available.

2 prepared strudel or phyllo sheets

1 cup melted butter

4 tablespoons unflavored bread crumbs

4 cooking apples, peeled, cored and thinly sliced

1 cup golden seedless raisins

1 cup raspberries, fresh, frozen or canned

1 cup chopped apricots, fresh or canned

$\frac{1}{4}$ cup chopped unsalted roasted almonds

$\frac{1}{4}$ cup chopped walnuts

$\frac{1}{2}$ cup sugar

2 teaspoons cinnamon

2 teaspoons pure vanilla extract

$\frac{1}{4}$ cup confectioner's sugar

Preheat the oven to 400°F. Spread one strudel sheet on a clean, lightly floured work surface. Brush the strudel sheet with half of the melted butter and sprinkle with 2 tablespoons of the breadcrumbs. Spread the second strudel sheet on top of the first. Brush the sheet with the remaining butter and sprinkle it with the remaining breadcrumbs.

♦ Combine the apples, raisins, raspberries, apricots, almonds, walnuts, cinnamon and vanilla extract in a mixing bowl. (If canned fruit is used, drain the syrup first.) Spread the mixture evenly over the surface of the top strudel sheet, leaving an inch border along each side. Roll up the strudel sheets like a jelly roll.

♦ Place the strudel on a greased baking sheet. Bake at 400°F for 30 minutes, then reduce the heat to 325°F for another 35 minutes. Cool for 30 minutes before slicing. Sprinkle with confectioner's sugar and serve.

German Austrian Festival Dinner

The menu below is one that might have been served in around 1900 in a Jewish home in Salzburg on a secular holiday such as New Year's Day or the Emperor's birthday. It could also have been served as a formal Sunday dinner. There is no appetizer or soup course because the dinner is very rich.

Wiener Schnitzel

Spaetzle with Roast Duck

Apple-Carrot Tzimmes

Hot Potato Salad

Brussels Sprouts Viennese

Fruit Compote

♦

Wiener Schnitzel

SERVES 6

One of the most famous of Austrian dishes, Wiener Schnitzel is best made from veal scallops or cutlets.

3 pounds very thin veal scallops
1½ cups lemon juice
½ teaspoon salt
1 teaspoon black pepper
1 tablespoon Worcestershire sauce
3 eggs, beaten
2 cups breadcrumbs
1 cup vegetable oil

In a deep bowl, marinate the veal scallops in the lemon juice for 1 hour.

♦ Drain the scallops well and pat dry with paper towels. Sprinkle the scallops with the salt, pepper and Worcestershire sauce. Dip the scallops first in the beaten egg, then in the breadcrumbs, then in the egg again and finally in the breadcrumbs. The scallops should be evenly coated.

♦ In a large, heavy skillet, heat the oil over a medium heat. Add the scallops and cook for 4 to 5 minutes on each side, or until they are crisp and golden brown. Serve garnished with lemon wedges.

Spaetzle with Roast Duck

SERVES 6

Spaetzle or spätzen are an extremely popular form of egg noodle. They go well with any sort of roast meat, but particularly with roast duck.

2-3 pound duck, split and cleaned, with the fat retained
4 cups flour
2 teaspoons salt
5 eggs
2 cups cold water
¼ cup lemon juice
½ cup orange juice
3 tablespoons currant or blackberry preserves
½ teaspoon black pepper

Preheat the oven to 325°F. Place the duck halves, skin-side up, in a roasting pan. Roast the duck for 1 hour.

♦ While the duck cooks, make the spaetzle. Place the flour in a large mixing bowl. Make a well in the center of the mound. Sprinkle 1 teaspoon of the salt in the well. Break the eggs into the well and mix them into the flour. Gradually add the water (more or less as needed) and mix to form a stiff dough.

♦ Turn the dough out onto a lightly floured work surface and knead it vigorously until it is smooth and elastic. Roll or shape the dough into narrow strips. With a sharp knife, cut the strips into tiny pieces.

♦ Bring 3 quarts water to a furious boil in a very large pot. Drop the spaetzle into the water. (Since each spaetzle must be able to float to the top of the water as it cooks, you may prefer to cook them in two or more pots of boiling water.) After the spaetzle rise to the top, boil for a further 15 minutes. Drain the spaetzle well and set them aside.

♦ After the duck has roasted for 1 hour, drain off the drippings, reserving ¼ cup.

♦ In a small bowl, combine the lemon juice, orange juice, preserves and pepper. Brush the skin of the duck with the mixture. Return the duck halves to the oven, skin-side up, and roast for 1 hour longer, draining off the drippings from the pan twice during the cooking time.

♦ With a sharp knife, remove all the skin and meat from the duck halves and shred them coarsely. Discard the bones. Put the shredded meat and skin into a large serving bowl.

♦ Bring 3 quarts of water to a furious boil in a large pot. Return the cooked spaetzle to the water for 1 minute. Drain the spaetzle well and add them to the shredded duck. Add the reserved duck drippings and salt to taste. Toss well and serve hot.

Apple-Carrot Tzimmes

SERVES 6

Tzimmes means mixture in Yiddish. The sweet and tangy flavor of the tzimmes is a good contrast to the richness of the Spaetzle with Roast Duck. Although served year round, this dish is traditional on Rosh Hashana. The sweetness symbolizes the hope for a sweet new year; the round carrot slices symbolize the hope for prosperity.

5 cups carrots, thinly sliced

2 dessert apples, peeled, cored and chopped

$\frac{1}{2}$ cup margarine

$\frac{1}{2}$ cup water

$\frac{1}{2}$ cup seedless white grapes

3 tablespoons honey

1 tablespoon brown sugar

$\frac{1}{2}$ teaspoon cinnamon

$\frac{1}{4}$ teaspoon nutmeg

Combine all the ingredients in a small saucepan. Simmer over a very low heat for 90 minutes. Add more water as needed if the mixture starts to dry out. Serve hot.

Hot Potato Salad

SERVES 6 TO 8

This hearty potato salad will come as a delightful surprise to those who think that potato salad can only be served cold.

$\frac{1}{4}$ pound corned or salt beef, shredded

$\frac{1}{4}$ pound pastrami, shredded

$\frac{1}{2}$ cup white wine vinegar

1 cup water

2 tablespoons sugar

2 teaspoons salt

1 teaspoon black pepper

8 cups cooked potatoes, peeled and cubed

$\frac{1}{2}$ cup chopped fresh parsley

1 teaspoon dried dill

Sauté half the corned beef and pastrami in a large skillet for 2 minutes. Add the vinegar, water, sugar, salt and pepper. Bring the liquid to a boil and cook, uncovered, for 10 minutes. Add the potatoes and cook for a further 8 minutes. Mix in the remaining corned beef and pastrami, and the parsley and dill. Serve hot.

Brussels Sprouts Viennese

SERVES 6

The unexpected addition of sweet red peppers gives this dish added zest. Use only fresh Brussels sprouts, and be careful not to overcook them.

1 pound fresh Brussels sprouts

1 sweet red pepper, seeded and cut into thin strips

4 tablespoons margarine or butter

1 teaspoon sesame seeds

Cook the Brussels sprouts in a large saucepan of salted boiling water until they are tender but not mushy, about 5 to 8 minutes. Remove the Brussels sprouts from the water with a slotted spoon and drain well.

♦ Add the red pepper strips to the pan and cook until they are tender but still crisp, about 2 minutes. Drain well.

♦ Toss the Brussels sprouts and red pepper strips together in a serving bowl.

♦ Melt the margarine or butter in a small saucepan over a low heat. Add the sesame seeds and cook for 1 minute, stirring constantly. Pour the mixture over the Brussels sprouts and red pepper. Toss well. Serve hot.

Fruit Compote

SERVES 8

Apart from baked dishes, no dessert is so completely identified with the German-Austrian tradition as fruit compote.

$\frac{1}{2}$ pound dried pears

$\frac{1}{2}$ pound dried apricots

$\frac{1}{2}$ pound dried peaches

$\frac{1}{2}$ cup dark raisins

$\frac{1}{2}$ cup golden seedless raisins

1 cup dried prunes, pitted

2 cups sugar

1 cinnamon stick

rind of 1 lemon, cut into thin strips

Soak the dried fruits overnight in a large bowl with enough cold water to cover the fruit to the depth of at least 2 inches.

♦ Pour the fruit soaking water into a large saucepan. Add the sugar, cinnamon and lemon rind. Bring the liquid to a boil over a medium heat, stirring until the sugar dissolves.

♦ Add the drained dried fruit and simmer for 10 minutes. Remove the fruit with a slotted spoon, and set aside. Boil the syrup mixture vigorously for 5 minutes. Remove the syrup from the heat and spoon it over the fruits immediately, while it is still hot. Chill thoroughly before serving.

German Austrian Sauerbraten Dinner

A traditional sauerbraten dinner is typical of German-Jewish fare from Vienna to Berlin. It is a hearty meal, ideal for staving off the cold in winter. To serve the sauerbraten on a Friday night, preparation should begin on the Monday before.

Lentil Soup
Beets with Horseradish
Sauerbraten
Sour Potatoes with Pickles
Berry Pudding

♦

Lentil Soup

SERVES 8

Like their Gentile counterparts, the Jews of Germany and Austria have always been fond of lentils and legumes in general. In a house of means, this hearty soup would serve as a substantial first course. In a poorer household, it might be the entire meal, served with boiled potatoes and dark bread.

3 cups dried lentils

3 quarts cold water

$\frac{1}{2}$ pound beef brisket, flank or stew meat

1 medium-sized leek, finely chopped

3 large carrots, finely chopped

1 parsnip, finely chopped

1 turnip, finely chopped

2 large celery stalks, finely chopped

$\frac{1}{4}$ cup beef fat

1 cup finely chopped onion

2 tablespoons flour

$\frac{1}{4}$ cup white wine

4 all-beef kosher frankfurters, cut into pieces

1 teaspoon salt

1 teaspoon black pepper

Rinse and sort the lentils under cold water. In a large casserole, bring the water to a boil. Add the lentils, beef, leek, carrots, parsnip, turnip and celery. Return the mixture to the boil, reduce the heat, cover and simmer for 40 minutes.

♦ Melt the beef fat in a large, heavy skillet over a low heat. When it is very hot, add the onions. Cook for 12 minutes, stirring frequently.

♦ Sprinkle the flour over the onions. Stir until the flour browns. Pour 1 cup of the lentil mixture over the onions and stir vigorously. Add the white wine and cook 1 minute longer.

♦ Add the contents of the skillet with the lentils. Simmer for 30 minutes.

♦ Add the frankfurters, salt and pepper to the soup. Simmer for a further 10 minutes. Serve hot with fresh crusty bread or melba toast.

Beets with Horseradish

SERVES 6

The Germans and Austrians have probably found more uses for the humble red beets than anyone else on Earth. This dish is traditionally served with Sauerbraten or roasted game birds.

3 cups boiled red beets, sliced

2 small apples, peeled, cored and diced

1 teaspoon caraway seeds

4 teaspoons drained, prepared white horseradish

$\frac{1}{2}$ teaspoon ground coriander

$\frac{1}{2}$ cup red wine vinegar

2 tablespoons sugar

1 teaspoon salt

In a large serving bowl combine the beets and apples. Add the caraway seeds, horseradish and coriander.

♦ In a large saucepan combine the vinegar, sugar and salt. Stir until the sugar has dissolved. Simmer over a very low heat for 8 minutes. Pour the liquid over the beets and apple mixture. Mix gently but thoroughly. Leave it to cool at room temperature for 30 minutes. Chill for 12 hours before serving.

Sauerbraten

SERVES 8—10

There are as many different versions of Sauerbraten as there are localities in Germany and Austria. You need to begin this dish 5 days before you want to serve it.

4 pounds beef brisket
2 cups red wine vinegar
2 cups white wine
2 teaspoons whole cloves
1 teaspoon whole black peppercorns
2 bay leaves
2 small onions, coarsely chopped
3 garlic cloves, quartered
1 large seedless orange with peel, sliced
$\frac{1}{4}$ cup lemon juice
1 cup water
1 tablespoon salt
2 tablespoons vegetable shortening
1 cup whole cooked tomatoes
1 cup tomato paste

Place the beef brisket in a large bowl or deep dish. Cover it with the vinegar, wine, cloves, peppercorns, bay leaves, onion, garlic, orange slices, lemon juice and water. Cover the bowl or dish tightly. Refrigerate for 4 days, turning the meat over daily.

♦ On the fifth day, remove the meat from the marinade and pat dry with paper towels. Reserve the marinade. Melt the shortening in a large casserole or heavy pot. Add the meat and brown well on all sides. Add the tomatoes, tomato paste and reserved marinade. Cover tightly and simmer for $2\frac{1}{2}$ hours, or until the meat is tender.

♦ Remove the meat from the casserole or pot and leave it to stand for ten minutes before slicing.

♦ Strain 3 cups of the cooking liquid through a sieve into a saucepan. Discard any solids remaining in the sieve. Bring the liquid to a boil and simmer for 5 minutes. Serve this as gravy with the sliced sauerbraten.

Sour Potatoes with Pickles

SERVES 6—8

All the vegetables in a traditional Sauerbraten should take on, to a greater or lesser degree, the tangy flavor of the main course. This uniquely Austrian recipe for potatoes should be made on the day the meal is served. The sourer the pickles, the better the dish.

6 large potatoes

2 tablespoons lemon juice

$\frac{1}{4}$ pound steak

2 cups beef broth

$\frac{1}{2}$ cup Spanish or red onion, diced

2 tablespoons flour

$\frac{1}{4}$ teaspoon dried marjoram

$\frac{1}{2}$ teaspoon salt

$\frac{1}{2}$ teaspoon black pepper

$\frac{1}{2}$ teaspoon dried parsley

$\frac{1}{4}$ teaspoon dried thyme

1 large bay leaf

3 sour pickles, finely chopped

Scrub the potatoes and cook them in a large pot of boiling water for 15 minutes, or until the potatoes are tender but not mushy. Drain well. Cut the potatoes into medium-sized chunks and put them into a serving bowl. Sprinkle the potatoes with the lemon juice and set aside.

♦ In a medium-sized heavy skillet, brown the steak in $\frac{1}{2}$ cup of the beef broth for about 2 minutes. Add the onions and flour and brown over a low heat for 10 minutes. Turn off the heat.

♦ Remove the steak and cut it into small pieces. Return the steak pieces to the skillet. Add the remaining beef broth and the marjoram, salt, pepper, parsley, thyme, bay leaf and pickles. Stir well. Cover the skillet and simmer for 30 minutes.

♦ Pour the mixture over the potatoes. Toss well and serve.

Berry Pudding

SERVES 8

This deliciously light dessert is a good way to end a heavy meal. The berries can be varied with the season.

$1\frac{1}{2}$ pounds fresh or frozen raspberries

$1\frac{1}{2}$ pounds fresh or frozen strawberries

2 cups fresh or canned peaches, finely chopped

$\frac{1}{4}$ cup Triple Sec or other orange-flavored liqueur

2 egg whites

If you are using frozen berries, thaw them first and drain well. If you are using fresh peaches, peel them and remove the pits. If you are using canned peaches, drain well. Purée the raspberries and strawberries in a blender or food processor.

♦ Beat the egg whites in a mixing bowl until they are stiff. Add the liqueur. Beat for a further 30 seconds. Add the berry purée to the egg white mixture. Mix gently until the purée is evenly distributed.

♦ Half fill 8 dessert glasses with the berry mixture. Spoon in a layer of diced peaches. Top with more berry mixture. Chill for 1 hour before serving.

German Austrian Dairy Lunch

The German and Austrian Jews showed a particular affinity in their cuisine for nearly all varieties of permitted fish. The menu below makes use of both pike and herring, and features the unusual accompaniment of red cabbage with apples. The chocolate pear dessert is a speciality of Berlin.

German Herring Salad
Baked Stuffed Pike
Red Cabbage with Apples
Green Bean Salad
Chocolate Pears

German Herring Salad

SERVES 6

This piquant herring salad is a delicious way to start a dairy meal. Serve it on a bed of lettuce with thin rounds of crusty bread.

14-16 ounces herring fillets

½ cup cooked beets, diced

3 scallions (including tops), diced

2 tablespoons white wine vinegar

½ teaspoon dried tarragon

½ teaspoon dried dill

2 tablespoons olive oil

¼ cup lemon juice

½ teaspoon black pepper

¼ cup orange juice

1 tablespoon Dijon-style mustard

Combine all the ingredients in a blender or food processor and chop finely. Spoon the salad into a serving bowl, cover tightly and refrigerate for at least 1 hour before serving.

Baked Stuffed Pike

SERVES 6

Pike is one of the finest of freshwater fish. This recipe, which originated in the Baden area of Germany, is a favorite among German Jews.

1 cup finely chopped onions

6 tablespoons melted butter

3 fresh garlic cloves, diced

1 cup finely chopped mushrooms

1 cup seasoned breadcrumbs

¼ cup milk

6 anchovies, ground to a paste

1 tablespoon capers

2 tablespoons finely chopped parsley

¼ cup grated Parmesan cheese

4 pound yellow pike, cleaned and scaled, without backbone, but with head and tail left intact

½ cup soured cream

1 teaspoon salt

1 teaspoon black pepper

3 tablespoons lemon juice

Prepare the stuffing first. In a medium-sized skillet, brown the onions in the butter. Cook for 2 to 3 minutes. Stir in the mushrooms and cook for a further 5 minutes.
♦ In a large mixing bowl, combine the breadcrumbs, milk, anchovies, capers, parsley and Parmesan cheese. Mix thoroughly. Set the stuffing aside.
♦ Preheat the oven to 425°F. Rinse the fish inside and out, and pat completely dry. Fill the cavity of the fish with the stuffing. Pour the butter, mushrooms and onions

over the fish. Bake the fish for 45 to 50 minutes, basting with the pan juices every 5 to 7 minutes.

◆ While the fish is cooking, combine the soured cream, salt, pepper and lemon juice in a small bowl. Chill.

◆ Remove the fish from the oven. Remove the stuffing from the cavity of the fish and place it in a large mixing bowl. Add half the fish drippings and half the onions and mushrooms from the baking pan. Mix well. Put the stuffing back into the fish. Reduce the oven temperature to 250°F. Return the fish to the oven for 5 minutes.

◆ Pour the remaining fish drippings, along with the remaining mushrooms and onions from the baking pan into a small saucepan. Add the chilled soured cream, mix and cook over a low heat, stirring frequently until heated through. Do not allow the sauce to boil.

◆ Arrange the fish on a serving platter. Pour some of the sauce over the fish. Serve the remainder of the fish sauce separately.

Red Cabbage with Apples

SERVES 6

Red cabbage is a staple of the German-Austrian Jewish diet, much as potatoes are for the Irish. There are an infinite number of ways to prepare it. This recipe is traditionally served with dairy lunches. It is also often served at Chanuka.

> 1 large red cabbage, shredded
>
> 2 tablespoons sugar
>
> 1 teaspoon salt
>
> 4 tablespoons butter
>
> $\frac{1}{2}$ cup raspberry vinegar
>
> 3 large cooking apples, peeled, cored and diced
>
> $\frac{1}{4}$ cup chopped scallions
>
> 1 bay leaf
>
> 1 whole clove
>
> 6 cups boiling water
>
> 4 tablespoons blackberry preserves
>
> $\frac{1}{4}$ cup dry red wine

In a large bowl, combine the shredded cabbage with the sugar, salt and vinegar. Toss until the cabbage is evenly coated with the vinegar mixture.

◆ In a large casserole, melt the butter. Add the apples and scallions and cook over a very low heat for 8 minutes, stirring frequently. Add the cabbage and vinegar mixture, the bay leaf and the clove. Stir in the boiling water. Cover and simmer over a low heat for 90 minutes.

◆ Add the blackberry preserves and red wine. Simmer for a further 30 minutes. Serve in a large glass or porcelain bowl.

Green Bean Salad

SERVES 6

This light salad is the perfect accompaniment to a hearty German-style dairy meal. It is particularly nice on hot summer days.

1½ pounds fresh green beans, trimmed and halved

For the dressing:

4 tablespoons olive oil

2 tablespoons white wine vinegar

¼ cup vegetable broth or water

½ teaspoon salt

1 teaspoon cayenne pepper

1 tablespoon finely chopped fresh dill or 1 teaspoon dried dill

2 teaspoons chopped fresh parsley

1 tablespoon Dijon-style mustard

Cook the green beans in a large pot of boiling water until they are tender but still crisp. Drain well. Put the green beans into a large serving bowl.

♦ In a mixing bowl combine the olive oil, vinegar, broth or water, salt, cayenne pepper, dill, parsley and mustard. Mix well.

♦ Pour the dressing over the green beans and toss well. Chill for 1 hour before serving.

Chocolate Pears

SERVES 6

This unique dessert originated in Bavaria, near the Austrian border. It should be served immediately.

For the chocolate sauce:

4 ounces semi-sweet chocolate

⅔ cup corn syrup

2 tablespoons margarine

For the dessert:

32 ounces canned pear halves, drained

2 pints whipping cream

½ cup sugar

1 pint vanilla ice-cream

First make the chocolate sauce. Place the chocolate, corn syrup and margarine in a bowl over a saucepan of hot water. As the chocolate and syrup melt, beat the mixture until it is smooth.

♦ Line the bottom of a large glass bowl with the pears. Pour ½ cup of the chocolate sauce over the pears.

♦ Whip the cream and sugar together until the mixture is soft and velvety. Spoon half the whipped cream over the pears.

♦ Spoon small pieces of the ice-cream over the whipped cream. Top with the remaining whipped cream. Drizzle the remaining chocolate sauce over the dessert and serve immediately. Garnish with lady fingers or sweet tea cookies.

Wiener Schnitzel ABOVE *is one of the most famous*
of Austrian dishes (page 134).
◆
Brussels Sprouts Viennese BELOW *is a colorful and*
tasty vegetable dish (page 136).

Apple-Carrot Tzimmes has a sweet and sour flavor that provides an excellent contrast to the richness of Spaetzle with Roast Duck at a German Austrian Festival Dinner (page 135).

Lentil Soup ABOVE LEFT *makes a substantial first course at a Sauerbraten Dinner (page 138).*

◆

Sour Potatoes with Pickles ABOVE RIGHT *provides a tangy accompaniment to Sauerbraten (page 140).*

◆

Chocolate Pears BELOW *is a unique dessert originating in Bavaria (page 144).*

France and Italy

FRANCE The Jewish communities of Marseilles, Aix, Arles, Avignon, Nîmes, Narbonne and other cities in Provence flourished from 800 on. They were principally trading communities, doing business with Egypt, Syria, India, China and Persia. Other Jewish communities were founded in Paris, Troyes, Nice, Bordeaux, Bayonne and Lyons. From the tenth to the thirteenth centuries, France was a major center of Jewish learning. Rashi (1040-1105), the greatest of Talmudic scholars, lived in Troyes. Many Jews emigrated to the Alsace region and the cities of Strasbourg, Metz, Verdun and Nancy to escape persecution in Germany from 1100 to 1500. Under Napoleon, French Jews were granted full citizenship, and many rose to prominence in government and business. Many Jews emigrated to France from North Africa, during the period of French control there.

During World War II some 100,000 French Jews were exterminated. The population has grown rapidly since, however, and today 700,000 Jews, half the Jewish population in Europe, live in France. Nearly half live in Paris, with the rest chiefly in Marseilles, Lyons, Nice, Toulon and Strasbourg. There are more than two hundred synagogues in France and more than fifty kosher restaurants. The Jewish area of the Marais district of Paris is called the Pletzel, and Jews have lived there since the eleventh century.

French-Jewish cooking is an interesting blend of Eastern European and Continental cuisine. The more assimilated Jews frequently ignored the kosher laws, but other simply modified standard French dishes to meet their dietary requirements. A kosher version of bouillabaisse is included here, a dish that is traditionally made with shellfish.

ITALY The word ghetto is derived from the Italian, where it first referred to the Jewish quarter of Venice. In fact, Jews have lived in Italy since Roman times. They developed highly successful communities renowned for their scholarship, and the first Hebrew book was printed in Italy in 1475. Jews in Italy traditionally enjoyed a great deal of liberty and freedom from persecution, although many were killed during World War II.

Italian Jewish cooking is a distinct branch of Italian cooking, just as, say, Sicilian cooking is. There are Jewish restaurants in Milan and Rome. Fried Artichokes Jewish-Style are as synonymous with Jewish cuisine in Italy as Chopped Liver is in the English-speaking world.

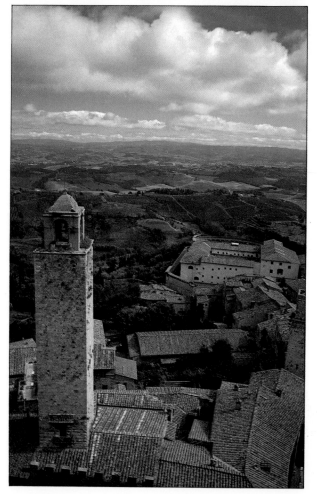

The Jews who settled in France and Italy adapted many of the classic dishes they found there to kosher requirements.

Baby Lamb ABOVE is traditionally served at an
Italian Passover Dinner (page 164).
♦
Jewish Artichokes BELOW is one of the most
famous of Italian Jewish dishes (page 165).

French Jewish Supper

Many French Jews contend that Jewish chefs had a profound influence on the style of classic French cuisine that reached its peak in the late nineteenth century. Below is a menu reminiscent of that period. It contains the famous Pâté Rothschild.

Pâté Rothschild

Vegetable Garlic Basil Soup

Braised Veal Chops

Braised Peas with Onions

and Lettuce

Stuffed Mushrooms Provençal

Soufflé Grand Marnier

Pâté Rothschild

SERVES 6—8

The House of Rothschild, world-famous for its financiers and philanthropists, began in Frankfurt in the sixteenth century. The family home was in the Judengasse (Jew Street), identified by a red shield, from which the family took its name. The five sons of Mayer Amschel Rothschild established branches of the family business in Germany, Austria, England, Italy and France. They were as well-known for their philanthropic work for Jewish causes as they were for their fabulous wealth.

1 pound fresh chicken livers, finely chopped

1 pound fresh calf's liver, finely chopped

2 eggs, beaten

$\frac{1}{2}$ cup cooked white beans, mashed

2 tablespoons lemon juice

4 tablespoons non-dairy cream substitute

1 garlic clove, finely chopped

1 bay leaf, crumbled

$\frac{1}{4}$ teaspoon salt

$\frac{1}{4}$ teaspoon black pepper

$\frac{1}{2}$ cup melted chicken fat

$\frac{1}{4}$ cup brandy

$\frac{1}{4}$ cup dark sherry

Preheat the oven to 325°F. Combine all the ingredients in a large wooden mixing bowl and mix thoroughly.
♦ Pack the pâté mixture into a small loaf pan. Smooth the top. Bake for 1½ hours.
♦ Remove the pâté from the oven and leave it to cool. Invert the loaf pan and turn out the pâté. Cover and chill for at least 3 hours before serving.

Vegetable Garlic Basil Soup

SERVES 8

This hearty traditional French soup can be a meal in itself. Serve with crusty bread.

5 tablespoons olive oil

1 cup finely chopped onions

5 garlic cloves, finely chopped

$2\frac{1}{2}$ quarts water

$\frac{1}{2}$ cup cooked white beans

1 pound fresh tomatoes, peeled, seeded and coarsely chopped

1 cup coarsely chopped carrots

1 cup diced new potatoes

$\frac{1}{4}$ cup finely chopped scallions

$\frac{1}{2}$ cup coarsely chopped celery, including leaves

1 cup trimmed fresh green beans, quartered

1 cup thinly sliced zucchini

4 tablespoons dried basil

2 tablespoons tomato paste

$\frac{1}{2}$ teaspoon salt

$\frac{1}{2}$ teaspoon black pepper

Heat 2 tablespoons olive oil in a large saucepan. Add the onions and garlic and sauté over a low heat for 5 minutes. Add the remaining ingredients, including the remaining olive oil, and simmer over a medium heat for 30 minutes, stirring occasionally. Serve hot.

Braised Veal Chops with Parsley Dressing

SERVES 6–8

These braised veal chops exemplify the subtle flavors of French Jewish cuisine.

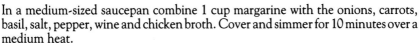

1 cup + 1 tablespoon margarine

1 cup finely chopped onions

$\frac{1}{2}$ cup finely chopped carrots

1 teaspoon dried basil

$\frac{1}{2}$ teaspoon salt

$\frac{1}{2}$ teaspoon black pepper

1$\frac{1}{2}$ cups white wine

1 cup chicken broth

4 tablespoons vegetable oil

1 cup unflavored breadcrumbs

$\frac{1}{2}$ cup ground salt beef

1 teaspoon lemon juice

3 tablespoons finely chopped parsley

8 loin veal chops, 1 inch thick

In a medium-sized saucepan combine 1 cup margarine with the onions, carrots, basil, salt, pepper, wine and chicken broth. Cover and simmer for 10 minutes over a medium heat.
♦ Heat the vegetable oil in a small skillet. Add the breadcrumbs and brown for 3 to 5 minutes over a low heat. Stir in the salt beef, lemon juice, parsley and the 1 tablespoon margarine. Cook over a low heat, stirring frequently, for 2 to 3 minutes.
♦ In a large flameproof casserole, arrange the veal chops in a single layer. Pour the broth mixture over the chops, and then the seasoned breadcrumb mixture.
♦ Cover and cook over a medium heat for 40 minutes, or until the veal is tender.

Braised Peas with Onions and Lettuce

SERVES 6–8

This simple dish should be made with fresh peas, not frozen or canned.

1 small head soft lettuce, coarsely torn

3 cups fresh peas

2 cups small onions

$\frac{1}{4}$ cup coarsely chopped parsley

6 tablespoons margarine

$\frac{1}{2}$ cup water

$\frac{1}{2}$ teaspoon salt

$\frac{1}{2}$ teaspoon sugar

1 tablespoon olive oil

Combine all the ingredients in a medium-sized saucepan and toss to distribute evenly. Cover and simmer over a low heat for 5 minutes.
♦ Remove the lid and toss again. Simmer for a further 3 to 5 minutes and serve.

Stuffed Mushrooms Provençal

SERVES 6—8

An excellent side dish, these mushrooms can also be served as an appetizer.

45 to 50 large mushrooms, stems removed and set aside
¼ cup finely chopped scallions
¼ cup finely chopped shallots
2 cups finely chopped fresh spinach
2 tablespoons chopped parsley
4 tablespoons margarine
2 tablespoons flour
¼ cup white wine
3 tablespoons olive oil

Preheat the oven to 350°F. Finely chop the mushroom stems. In a small saucepan, combine the scallions, shallots, spinach, parsley, margarine, flour, white wine and olive oil. Mix thoroughly and cook over a low heat until the margarine melts. Cover and simmer for 2 minutes.

♦ Add the mushroom stems. Mix thoroughly and cover. Simmer the filling over a low heat for a further 5 minutes.

♦ Place approximately 1 teaspoon of the filling in each mushroom cap. Place the filled caps on greased baking sheets and bake for 15 minutes. Serve hot.

Soufflé Grand Marnier

SERVES 6—8

Grand Marnier, the famed orange-flavored liqueur, is the base for this delicious soufflé. The use of margarine instead of butter makes the soufflé pareve; butter could be used if the soufflé is to be served with a dairy meal.

10 egg yolks
1 cup sugar
½ cup Grand Marnier liqueur
1½ tablespoons grated orange peel
14 egg whites
½ teaspoon cream of tartar
4 tablespoons softened margarine
1½ tablespoons superfine sugar

Beat the egg yolks in the top of a double boiler. Gradually beat in 4 tablespoons of the sugar until the mixture is a light lemon colour.

♦ Fill the lower compartment of the double boiler halfway with water. Bring the water to a simmer and cook the egg yolk mixture over it, stirring gently until the mixture thickens and becomes very hot.

♦ Stir the liqueur and the orange peel into the egg yolk mixture. Pour the mixture into a medium-sized metal mixing bowl and chill in the freezer until very cold.

♦ Beat the egg whites and cream of tartar together in a large mixing bowl until they are stiff. Gently fold the egg yolk mixture into the egg whites.

♦ Preheat the oven to 425°F. Thoroughly grease a 3 quart soufflé dish with the softened margarine. Evenly sprinkle the sides and bottom of the dish with the remaining sugar. Spoon the soufflé mixture into the dish. Bake in the center of the oven for 3 minutes. Reduce the heat to 400°F and bake for a further 30 minutes, or until puffed and lightly browned. Sprinkle with the superfine sugar and serve immediately.

French Jewish Dairy Supper

This dairy meal includes kosher versions of two standards of French cuisine: Onion Soup and Fisherman's Stew, an adaptation of the famed Bouillabaisse.

Chopped Herring Marseilles
French Onion Soup
Fisherman's Stew with Rouille
Asparagus with Hollandaise Sauce
Raspberry Mousse
Chocolate Mousse

Chopped Herring Marseilles

SERVES 6—8

This French version of herring salad is a perfect first course for a dairy meal.

8 large salt herring fillets

½ cup finely chopped onion

2 apples, peeled, cored and finely chopped

3 hard-boiled eggs, finely chopped

4 tablespoons vinegar

3 slices white bread, trimmed and shredded

2 teaspoons sugar

2½ tablespoons olive oil

Soak the herring overnight in cold water in a large mixing bowl. Drain well and chop finely.

♦ In a mixing bowl combine the herring with the remaining ingredients. Mix thoroughly until the consistency is even throughout. Cover and chill for at least 4 hours before serving.

French Onion Soup

SERVES 8

Served in individual bowls topped with melted cheese, this soup is a French classic.

2 tablespoons vegetable oil

4 tablespoons butter

2 pounds onions, coarsely chopped

2 tablespoons flour

2 quarts vegetable broth

½ teaspoon salt

12 slices Swiss cheese

16 thin slices cut from a French stick loaf

2 teaspoons olive oil

2 garlic cloves, finely chopped

Heat the vegetable oil and butter in a large deep saucepan. Add the onions and sauté over a medium heat for 5 minutes. Reduce the heat to low and simmer for a further 20 minutes, stirring frequently.

♦ Sprinkle the onions with the flour and continue cooking, stirring constantly, for 3 minutes.

♦ Add the vegetable broth and salt. Simmer, covered, for 35 minutes over a low heat.

♦ While the soup simmers, coarsely chop 4 of the cheese slices. Preheat the oven to 325°F.

♦ Brush the bread slices with the olive oil and arrange them in a single layer on a baking sheet. Sprinkle the bread with the garlic and the chopped cheese. Bake for 15 minutes and set aside.

♦ When the soup is done, place 2 bread slices in each of 8 individual deep soup bowls or ramekins. Fill each bowl with soup and top with a slice of cheese. Place the bowls on the center rack of the oven and raise the heat to 350°F. Bake for 5 to 7 minutes or until the cheese begins to soften and turn brown. Remove the bowls from the oven, allow to cool for 1 minute and serve.

Fisherman's Stew with Rouille

SERVES 8

Bouillabaisse, the famous French fish stew, is made with both fish and shellfish. This kosher adaptation is made with fish alone. Like Bouillabaisse, it is served with rouille, a piquant condiment mixture that is added to each serving to taste.

2 pounds fresh halibut steaks

2 pound red snapper, cleaned

2 pound striped bass, cleaned

2 pounds haddock steaks

2 pounds cod-fish steaks

2 pounds pike steaks

2 pound whitefish, cleaned

9 tablespoons olive oil

2 cups onions, coarsely chopped

1 cup thinly sliced leeks

6 garlic cloves, finely chopped

7 cups water

2 cups white wine

3 pounds tomatoes, peeled, seeded and coarsely chopped

1 teaspoon grated orange peel

1 teaspoon dried thyme

1 tablespoon roughly chopped parsley

1 bay leaf

$\frac{1}{4}$ teaspoon saffron threads

$\frac{1}{2}$ teaspoon salt

$\frac{1}{2}$ teaspoon black pepper

2 green peppers, coarsely chopped

$\frac{1}{2}$ teaspoon Tabasco sauce

$\frac{1}{2}$ cup chopped pimento

3 tablespoons unflavored breadcrumbs

5 cups cooked rice

Trim the skin and bones from the fish steaks. Fillet the whole fish. Cut the fish steaks and fillets into 1 inch cubes. Reserve the trimmings, heads and bones.

♦ Heat 3 tablespoons of the olive oil in a large, 6 quart saucepan. Add the onions, leeks and 2 chopped garlic cloves. Cook over a low heat, stirring occasionally, for 5 minutes.

♦ Add 6 cups of the water and the white wine and reserved fish trimmings to the pan. Cover and simmer over a low heat for 5 minutes.

♦ Add the tomatoes, orange rind, thyme, parsley, bay leaf, saffron, salt and pepper. Raise the heat slightly and simmer, covered, for 15 minutes. Remove the cover and simmer for a further 10 minutes.

♦ Prepare the rouille. Combine the remaining garlic with the green peppers, Tabasco sauce, pimentos, remaining olive oil and breadcrumbs. Mix well.

♦ Put the rouille mixture into a saucepan and add 1 cup water. Simmer over a moderate heat for 10 minutes. Put the rouille into a serving bowl and set aside.

♦ When the fish broth is ready, strain it through a cheesecloth into another saucepan. Discard the solids remaining in the cheesecloth.

♦ Bring the strained broth to a boil over a medium heat. Add the fish pieces and cook for 10 minutes. Reduce the heat to low and cook for a further 5 minutes.

♦ Put $\frac{1}{2}$ cup of the cooked rice into each individual soup bowl. Ladle the soup on top. Serve with rouille.

Asparagus with Hollandaise Sauce

SERVES 8

When making Hollandaise sauce, never let the sauce boil, or it will curdle. Use the thinnest, freshest asparagus you can find.

2 pounds thin green asparagus
12 tablespoons butter
3 egg yolks
1 tablespoon lemon juice
1 tablespoon heavy cream
$\frac{1}{4}$ teaspoon salt
$\frac{1}{4}$ teaspoon ground white pepper

Fill a medium-sized saucepan to a depth of 3 inches with water.
♦ Add the asparagus, cover and simmer over a medium heat for 12 minutes.
♦ Meanwhile, melt the butter in a small saucepan and set aside, keeping the butter warm over a very low heat.
♦ In a small mixing bowl, beat the egg yolks and lemon juice together for 3 to 5 minutes, or until the mixture thickens.
♦ Beat the egg yolk mixture into the melted butter over a very low heat. Beat in the cream, salt and white pepper. Remove from the heat and let the sauce thicken for 5 minutes, stirring gently but frequently.
♦ Drain the cooked asparagus well and place in a large deep serving dish. Top with the Hollandaise sauce. Serve warm.

Raspberry Mousse

SERVES 6—8

Frozen raspberries can be used in this adaptation of the traditional French recipe.

2 cups fresh raspberries
4 egg yolks, beaten
$\frac{1}{2}$ cup water
1 teaspoon arrowroot
$\frac{3}{4}$ cup sugar
$\frac{1}{4}$ cup framboise or blackberry liqueur
2 cups heavy cream
1 tablespoon vegetable oil

Crush the raspberries and push them through a fine sieve into a bowl. Discard any solids that remain in the sieve.
♦ In a small saucepan, combine the beaten egg yolks with the water and arrowroot. Stir briskly over a medium heat and gradually add the sugar, stirring until it is completely dissolved. Add the crushed raspberries and the liqueur. Stir well, cover and cook over a low heat for 5 minutes.
♦ In a large mixing bowl, whip the cream until it is stiff.
♦ Gradually spoon the heated raspberry mixture into the cream, stirring constantly until they are thoroughly combined.
♦ With the vegetable oil grease a large pudding mold. Pour the raspberry mousse into the mold. Freeze the mousse until it is solid. Remove from the freezer and leave it to thaw for 1 hour before serving.

Chocolate Mousse

SERVES 8

One of the most famous of French desserts, Chocolate Mousse takes quite a long time to make.

> 8 egg yolks
>
> $\frac{3}{4}$ cup superfine sugar
>
> $1\frac{1}{2}$ tablespoons brandy
>
> $1\frac{1}{2}$ tablespoons Triple Sec liqueur
>
> 12 ounces semi-sweet chocolate, crumbled
>
> $3\frac{1}{2}$ tablespoons strong coffee
>
> 1 pound sweet butter, softened
>
> 8 egg whites
>
> $1\frac{1}{2}$ cups heavy cream

In a large flameproof mixing bowl, beat the egg yolks, $\frac{1}{2}$ cup sugar, brandy and Triple Sec into a pale frothy mixture.

♦ Set the bowl over a saucepan of simmering water and continue beating for 6 minutes, or until the mixture is hot.

♦ Place the bowl inside a larger bowl filled with crushed ice and beat for 5 minutes, or until the mixture has a thick creamy consistency. Set aside.

♦ Melt the chocolate pieces with the coffee in a small saucepan over a low heat. When the chocolate has completely melted, beat in the softened butter until the mixture thickens and is smooth and even.

♦ Spoon the chocolate mixture into the egg yolk mixture and beat gently until creamy.

♦ In another bowl, beat the egg whites until they are stiff. Gradually fold them into the chocolate mixture. Cover the bowl and chill.

♦ In a medium-sized metal mixing bowl, whip the cream together with the remaining sugar until it has a soft but fairly firm consistency.

♦ Spoon the chocolate mousse into tulip dessert glasses and top with the whipped cream. Chill before serving.

Italian Passover Dinner

The Italian Jews have developed a cuisine that is as distinct from the rest of Italian cooking as 'Jewish food' is in Britain and the United States. In fact, in the large Italian cities there are restaurants serving Jewish specialties just as there are Jewish delis in other countries. Italian Jewish food is quite different from what even a French Jew would consider Jewish cooking.

Passover Chicken Soup

Striped Bass in Jelly

Sautéed Spinach

Baby Lamb

Jewish Artichokes

Matzoh Omelette

Passover Chicken Soup

SERVES 8

This delicious soup is the traditional first course at a Passover meal in Italy.

1 chicken breast, skinned and boned, and finely chopped
1 egg, beaten
$\frac{1}{4}$ cup matzoh meal
3 tablespoons water
$\frac{1}{4}$ teaspoon salt
$\frac{1}{4}$ teaspoon grated nutmeg
$\frac{1}{4}$ teaspoon ground cinnamon
$2\frac{1}{2}$ quarts chicken broth
$\frac{1}{2}$ cup rice
8 hard-boiled egg yolks

In a large mixing bowl, combine the chopped chicken meat with the egg, matzoh meal, water, salt, nutmeg and cinnamon. Mix well. Cover the mixing bowl and chill for 30 minutes.

◆ Shape the chicken mixture into small balls approximately $\frac{3}{4}$ inch in diameter. In a large saucepan, bring the broth to a boil over a high heat. Add the rice and chicken balls. Reduce the heat to medium and cover. Simmer for 20 minutes.

◆ Place one hard-boiled egg yolk in the centre of each of eight deep soup bowls. Ladle the soup over the top. Serve hot.

Striped Bass in Jelly

SERVES 6—8

This Italian specialty is similar to the more familiar gefilte fish.

1 pound striped bass
1 cup diced onion
1 cup diced celery
$\frac{1}{2}$ cup sliced carrots
1 tablespoon lemon juice
$\frac{1}{2}$ teaspoon ground white pepper
$\frac{1}{2}$ teaspoon salt
3 cups cold water

Clean and fillet the fish. Reserve the head and bones. In a medium-sized saucepan, place the fish fillets, reserved head and bones, onion, celery, carrots, lemon juice, pepper, salt and water. Simmer over a low heat for 20 minutes.

◆ Carefully remove the pieces of fish fillet with a slotted spoon and place them in a deep medium-sized glass or ceramic, but not metal, dish. Cover and chill.

◆ Strain the broth through a fine sieve. Discard the solids remaining in the sieve. Return the broth to the pan and bring to a boil over a high heat. Cook for 15 to 20 minutes, or until the liquid is reduced by about half.

◆ Pour the broth over the fish pieces and chill for two hours or more. The broth will gel as it chills. Serve cold with mayonnaise and/or lemon wedges.

Sautéed Spinach

SERVES 6—8

It is customary in Italy to serve a green vegetable dish halfway through dinner. This spinach dish is traditional at Passover.

3 pounds fresh spinach

3 garlic cloves, quartered

½ cup olive oil

¼ teaspoon salt

¼ teaspoon black pepper

Remove any tough stems and blemished leaves from the spinach. Rinse the spinach thoroughly to remove all grit. Drain well.

♦ In a large, heavy skillet, brown the garlic in the olive oil over a low heat. Add the spinach leaves, salt and pepper. Cook for 10 minutes, stirring frequently. Serve immediately.

Baby Lamb

SERVES 8

This dish is traditionally made with chops from a young goat, an animal that is kosher. But the recipe is often adapted to lamb, which is more easily available.

4 pounds lamb rib chops

3 tablespoons olive oil

½ teaspoon salt

¼ teaspoon black pepper

¼ cup coarsely chopped parsley

2 garlic cloves, finely chopped

1½ cups cold water

2 egg yolks

2 tablespoons lemon juice

Place the lamb chops in a large heavy skillet. Add the oil, salt, pepper, parsley and garlic. Pour the water over the meat and spices, cover, and simmer over a low heat for 1 hour.

♦ In a small mixing bowl, combine the egg yolks and lemon juice. Pour over the lamb and cover. Simmer for another 3 minutes and serve.

Jewish Artichokes

SERVES 6—8

This artichoke dish is as closely identified with Jewish cooking in Italy as Chopped Liver is with Jewish cooking in the English-speaking world.

12 fresh artichokes, trimmed

1 tablespoon salt

1 tablespoon black pepper

3 cups olive oil

$\frac{1}{4}$ cup lemon juice

$\frac{1}{2}$ cup water

Sprinkle the artichokes with the salt and pepper, making sure that some of the seasoning finds its way between the individual leaves.

♦ Put the oil in a medium-sized saucepan. Place over a medium heat. Put as many artichokes in the pan, stem down, as will fit comfortably. Cook for 25 minutes. As the artichokes cook, sprinkle them periodically with the lemon juice and water until these are used up.

♦ After 25 minutes, carefully invert the artichokes, two at a time, in the oil. Remove when the leaves open and turn golden brown.

Matzoh Omelette

SERVES 8

This delicious omelette can be served as the dessert course at a Passover dinner, or on its own as a lunch or breakfast.

8 plain matzohs

12 eggs, beaten

$\frac{1}{2}$ teaspoon salt

$\frac{1}{4}$ cup pine kernels

$\frac{1}{2}$ cup golden seedless raisins

finely grated rind of 1 lemon

2 tablespoons vegetable oil

$\frac{1}{2}$ cup sugar

$1\frac{1}{2}$ teaspoon ground cinnamon

Soak the matzohs in water for 3 to 5 minutes or until soft. Drain well.

♦ In a large mixing bowl, combine the softened matzohs, eggs, salt, pine kernels, raisins and lemon rind. Mix well.

♦ Heat the vegetable oil in a large heavy skillet over a low heat.

♦ Pour the omelette mixture into the skillet and cover. Cook for 8 minutes or until the omelette is solid. Sprinkle with the sugar and cinnamon. Fold the omelette in half and remove from the pan. Serve warm.

Italian Chanuka Dinner

It is traditional in Italy for a Chanuka menu to include a variety of fried foods in commemoration of the sanctified oil that miraculously burned for eight days when the Temple in Jerusalem was rededicated in 165 BCE, after the Maccabees defeated the Syrians.

Crêpes with Tuna

Holiday Fried Chicken

Rice with Raisins

Chanuka Fritters

Crêpes with Tuna

SERVES 6—8

This unusual recipe is a Chanuka favorite with the Italian Jews. Use imported Italian tuna packed in oil for the best results.

2 × 6½ ounce cans Italian tuna, drained

2 ounce can anchovies, drained

2 tablespoons chopped parsley

½ teaspoon salt

½ teaspoon pepper

6 eggs, beaten

1 cup flour

1 cup cold water

2 teaspoons finely chopped onion

2 tablespoons vegetable oil

In a medium-sized mixing bowl, combine the tuna, anchovies, parsley, salt and pepper. Flake with a fork and mix until evenly blended. Set the filling aside.

◆ In another mixing bowl, combine the eggs, flour, water and onions. Mix the batter thoroughly.

◆ Lightly grease a large heavy skillet with the vegetable oil. Place over a medium heat. Ladle 3 tablespoons of the batter at a time into the skillet, spreading it evenly, and cook for 3 to 5 minutes or until the crêpe is solid but still slightly moist. Place 1 tablespoon of the tuna filling on the crêpe and fold it over. Remove from skillet and set aside on a large baking sheet. Repeat the process until all the batter and filling are used up.

◆ Preheat the oven to 450°F. Place the baking sheet in the oven and bake for 8 minutes. Serve hot.

Holiday Fried Chicken

SERVES 8

This Italian version of fried chicken also makes an excellent appetizer or buffet dish.

1 teaspoon salt

½ teaspoon black pepper

¼ teaspoon ground nutmeg

¼ teaspoon ground cinnamon

½ teaspoon finely chopped garlic

2 small chickens, cut into small pieces

3 tablespoons lemon juice

1 cup olive oil

1 cup flour

2 eggs, beaten

In a small mixing bowl, combine the salt, pepper, nutmeg, cinnamon and garlic. Mix well. Rub the chicken pieces with the mixture and then sprinkle them with the lemon juice.

◆ Heat the oil in a large heavy skillet over a moderate heat until it is very hot.

◆ Dip half the spiced chicken pieces in the flour and then in the egg. Sauté, turning frequently, for 20 minutes. Keep the pieces from this first batch in a warm oven while cooking the remainder. Serve hot with lemon wedges.

Rice with Raisins

SERVES 6—8

This traditional Italian Chanuka dish originated with the Jews of Venice.

4 tablespoons olive oil

2 cups rice

2 tablespoons finely chopped parsley

2 garlic cloves, finely chopped

$\frac{1}{4}$ cup dark seedless raisins

$\frac{1}{2}$ cup golden seedless raisins

$\frac{1}{4}$ teaspoon salt

$\frac{1}{4}$ teaspoon ground white pepper

4 cups chicken broth

In a large heavy skillet, heat the oil over a high heat. Add the rice, parsley, garlic and dark raisins. Cook for 5 minutes, stirring frequently.

♦ Add the golden raisins, salt, pepper and chicken broth. Cover and cook over a high heat for 20 minutes. Serve warm.

Chanuka Fritters

SERVES 8

This baked dessert is distinctly Jewish-Italian.

2 packages active dry yeast

1 cup tepid water

3 cups flour

$\frac{1}{2}$ teaspoon salt

1 cup golden seedless raisins

2 teaspoons anise seeds

$1\frac{1}{2}$ tablespoons olive oil

2 tablespoons lemon juice

2 cups honey

1 cup vegetable oil

In a small mixing bowl, dissolve the yeast in the tepid water. Leave it for 3 minutes.

♦ Add the yeast mixture to the flour, salt, raisins, anise seeds, olive oil, a scant tablespoon of the lemon juice and $\frac{1}{2}$ cup of the honey in a large mixing bowl. Mix with a wooden spoon into a soft dough.

♦ Place the dough on a floured surface and knead for 10 to 12 minutes or until the dough becomes elastic. Shape the dough into a ball and put it into an oiled bowl. Cover with a clean tea-towel and leave in a warm place for 1 hour. The dough will greatly increase in volume.

♦ using your hands, flatten the dough into a sheet $\frac{1}{2}$ inch thick and leave it to stand for 15 minutes. Cut the dough into approximately 36 to 40 squares.

♦ In a deep heavy skillet heat the vegetable oil over a medium heat until it is very hot. Add the dough squares, 6 at a time, and sauté until golden on each side, about 3 to 5 minutes per side.

♦ Remove the dough squares as they are done and drain them on paper towels.

♦ In a small saucespan, combine the remaining honey and lemon juice and bring to a boil over a medium heat. Cook for 3 minutes.

♦ Place the fritters in a large deep dish and pour the hot honey sauce over them. Serve immediately.

Italian
Yom Kippur Dinner

Yom Kippur, or the Day of Atonement, is a solemn fast day. A large meal is traditionally served before the holy "day" begins at sundown, and then a lighter, simpler meal is served to break the fast twenty-four hours later. Challah, the traditional Jewish egg bread would be served (see p.126 for a recipe). Dishes for both meals are given in this section.

Red Snapper Jewish-Style
Vegetable Cream Soup
Stewed Fennel
Cold Spaghetti with Brusco Sauce
Veal Scallops with Red Wine
Fried Chicory
Cinnamon Turnovers

Yom Kippur Bread

SERVES 8

This traditional loaf is served immediately after the holy day ends, to break the fast.

5½ cups flour

2 packages active dry yeast

1 cup tepid water

1½ cups sugar

3 eggs

½ cup olive oil

2 tablespoons anise seeds

3 teaspoons pure vanilla extract

1½ teaspoon salt

2 egg yolks

In a large mixing bowl, combine 2 cups of the flour with the yeast, water, and 2 tablespoons of the sugar. Mix with a whisk into a smooth dough. Sprinkle with ½ cup of the flour and cover the bowl with a clean tea-towel. Set aside for 2½ hours.
♦ Add the 3 whole eggs, remaining sugar, olive oil, anise seeds, vanilla extract, salt and remaining flour. Mix into an even dough.
♦ Knead the dough until stiff on a floured surface. Divide the dough in half and knead each half for an additional 5 minutes. Let the dough rest for 5 minutes.
♦ Shape the dough halves into two 10 inch loaves and place them on a greased and floured baking sheet. Cover with a clean tea-towel and leave for 1½ hours.
♦ Preheat the oven to 375°F. In a small mixing bowl, beat the egg yolks with 2 teaspoons of water and brush the mixture over the tops of the loaves. Bake for 30 minutes. Remove and leave them to cool on wire racks.

Red Snapper Jewish-style

SERVES 8

This simple but delicious recipe is traditionally served to break the Yom Kippur fast. It has been part of Italian-Jewish cuisine for hundreds of years.

1 large red snapper

¼ cup red wine vinegar

½ cup olive oil

1 cup white wine

2½ cups water

2 teaspoons sugar

1 teaspoon salt

2 garlic cloves, finely chopped

Clean and fillet the fish. Reserve the head and bones. In a saucepan, combine the reserved fish trimmings with the vinegar, olive oil, wine, water, sugar, salt and garlic. Cover and simmer over a low heat for 30 minutes.
♦ Strain the fish stock mixture through a fine sieve. Discard any solids that remain in the sieve.
♦ Preheat the oven to 425°F. Place the red snapper fillets in a large baking pan. Pour the fish stock mixture over the fillets. Bake for 30 minutes. Pour off the cooking liquid and serve in a gravy boat on the side. Serve hot.

Vegetable Cream Soup

SERVES 6

This delicious soup has a creamy texture yet uses no milk products.

$\frac{1}{4}$ cup olive oil

4 garlic cloves, finely chopped

1 onion, coarsely chopped

$\frac{1}{2}$ pound green beans, trimmed and quartered

1 cup peeled and coarsely chopped zucchini

1 cup peeled and coarsely chopped yellow squash

$\frac{1}{2}$ cup sliced carrots

1 cup peeled and cubed turnips

1 cup coarsely chopped celery

2 cups peeled and cubed potatoes

$\frac{1}{2}$ cup finely chopped leeks

$\frac{1}{2}$ cup finely chopped spinach

$\frac{1}{2}$ cup cooked baby peas

1 cup cooked lima beans

$\frac{1}{2}$ cup jellied cranberry sauce

$\frac{1}{4}$ cup finely chopped parsley

2 tablespoons coarsely chopped fresh basil

1 teaspoon salt

$\frac{1}{4}$ teaspoon ground white pepper

6 cups water

In a large saucepan, combine all the ingredients. Mash with a fork.
◆ Cover and 1immer for 40 minutes over a low heat. Mash again. Replace the lid and simmer for an additional 20 minutes over a low heat. Serve hot.

Stewed Fennel

SERVES 6—8

The anise-like flavor of fennel is popular with all Italians, both Jews and Gentiles.

3 large fennel bulbs

6 tablespoons olive oil

1 cup chopped onion

2 cups water

$\frac{1}{2}$ teaspoon salt

$\frac{1}{4}$ teaspoon black pepper

Trim the fronds from the fennel bulbs. Cut the bulbs in half vertically, then chop each half horizontally into slices.
◆ Heat the olive oil in a large heavy skillet. Add the fennel rings and onion and sauté over a low heat for 6 to 8 minutes. Stir frequently.
◆ Add the water, salt and pepper and raise the heat to medium. Cook for 25 to 30 minutes. Serve with the cooking liquid in a deep dish.

Cold Noodles with Brusco Sauce

SERVES 6—8

This pasta dish is made the day before Yom Kippur and served to break the fast.

1 pound thin spaghetti, cooked al dente

½ cup olive oil

2 garlic cloves, finely chopped

1 teaspoon dried rosemary

½ teaspoon dried sage

½ teaspoon salt

¼ teaspoon black pepper

1 egg

1 egg yolk

2 tablespoons lemon juice

1½ cups beef broth

Put the spaghetti in a large saucepan of boiling water and cook for about 5 minutes until *al dente*. Drain thoroughly.

♦ Combine all the ingredients except the spaghetti in a small skillet. Cook over a medium heat for 10 minutes, stirring occasionally. Reduce the heat to low and cook for an additional 5 minutes.

♦ Put the cooked spaghetti into a serving bowl. Pour the sauce over the spaghetti and toss well. Leave to stand for 10 minutes, stirring occasionally. Cover the bowl, chill for at least 1 hour and serve cold.

Veal Scallops with Red Wine

SERVES 8

These delicate and delicious veal scallops are quite simple to prepare.

½ cup flour

½ teaspoon salt

½ teaspoon ground white pepper

3 pounds thinly sliced veal scallops

8 tablespoons olive oil

2 large onions, coarsely chopped

3 garlic cloves, finely chopped

2 tablespoons coarsely chopped parsley

½ cup red wine

½ cup sweet sherry

2 cups water

¼ cup tomato paste

On a large ceramic plate mix the flour, salt and pepper together. Lightly dredge the veal slices in the mixture.

♦ Heat the olive oil in a large heavy skillet. Add the veal, onions and garlic and cook over a medium heat for 3 to 5 minutes, or until both sides of the veal slices are browned. Remove the veal slices and keep warm.

♦ Add the parsley, wine, sherry, water and tomato paste to the skillet. Stir well and bring to a boil over a high heat. Cook for 3 minutes. Cover and simmer for 10 minutes longer. Serve the sauce spooned over the veal scallops.

Fried Chicory

SERVES 8

This simple vegetable dish is a standard of Italian-Jewish cooking, and may have been borrowed by the Jews from the ancient Romans.

4 pounds chicory, washed and trimmed
1 teaspoon black pepper
1 cup olive oil

Cook the chicory in a large saucepan of boiling water for 5 minutes. Drain well. Sprinkle the chicory with the pepper.

♦ Heat the olive oil in a large heavy skillet over a medium heat. Add the chicory and sauté for about 10 to 12 minutes, until the chicory turns golden brown. Remove the leaves from the skillet and drain on paper towels. Serve warm.

Cinnamon Turnovers

SERVES 8

Light and flakey, these turnovers are fairly complicated to make. They would be served before the fast begins.

3 cups flour
$1\frac{1}{4}$ cups warm water
$\frac{1}{2}$ cup vegetable oil
1 teaspoon salt
$\frac{1}{2}$ cup softened margarine
2 cups sugar
2 tablespoons cinnamon
$1\frac{1}{2}$ tablespoons brandy
$1\frac{1}{2}$ tablespoons Triple Sec liqueur
$1\frac{1}{2}$ tablespoons water
2 egg yolks, beaten

In a medium-sized mixing bowl, combine the flour, warm water, vegetable oil and salt. Mix into a soft dough. Knead for 5 minutes and then set aside for 30 minutes.

♦ Roll the dough out on a floured surface into a sheet $\frac{1}{2}$ inch thick.

♦ Melt the margarine and let it cool to room temperature. Spread a thin layer of margarine on the dough and dust with flour.

♦ Fold the dough to one third of its size. Wrap in plastic wrap and chill for 20 minutes. Roll the dough out into a sheet as before. Repeat the process three more times, chilling the dough for 20 minutes each time. Roll the dough out into a sheet a final time.

♦ Cut the dough into 14 to 16 squares.

♦ In a small mixing bowl combine the sugar, cinnamon, brandy, Triple Sec and 2 tablespoons water.

♦ Brush the sugar mixture evenly over the dough squares. Roll up the squares diagonally, starting from one of the corners, into cylinders. Brush the egg yolks over the cylinders.

♦ Preheat the oven to 400°F. Place the cylinders on an ungreased baking sheet and bake for 20 minutes. Leave them to cool on a wire rack and serve at room temperature.

Spain, Portugal
and the New World

Spain and Portugal Jews first settled in Spain and Portugal in the first century CE. By the fourth century they were already beginning to suffer from discrimination. The Arab conquest of Spain in the eighth century was welcomed by the Jews, who subsequently enjoyed a period of enlightened prosperity. Toledo was the home of the largest and most influential Jewish community — by the twelfth century it numbered more than 12,000 members and had many synagogues. The city of Cordoba is remembered as the birthplace of one of the greatest Jewish literary figures, Moses Maimonides, who was born there in 1135. Jews also played an important role in Granada, Seville, the Costa del Sol, Madrid and Barcelona.

By the thirteenth century however, the Arab decline had begun and discrimination again arose. A pogrom in Seville in 1391 began a long period of persecution and enforced conversions, with many Jews in Spain unwillingly baptized and outwardly converted to Christianity. Many Jews continued to practise their own religion in secret, and were known by Christians as 'Marranos', from the Spanish word for 'damned'. From 1480 onwards, the Marranos became a target of the Spanish Inquisition — they were sought out and killed and in 1492 — the same year that Columbus opened the way to the New World — the Jewish community was officially outlawed from Spain and Portugal by the Edict of Expulsion. Tiny remnants remained, but 160,000 were forced to leave their homes.

The New World Many fled to Italy, Turkey, Morocco and elsewhere in the Mediterranean, and later further north to France and Holland. But from the start, Jews also found their way to the Spanish- and Portuguese-speaking parts of the New World. The first synagogue in the Americas was founded in Curaçao in 1651, and three years later the first Jewish community in North America was established in Nieuw Amsterdam, now New York City. Thus the world-wide dispersion of Sephardic Jews was brought about — Sephardic comes from *Sephardim*, the Hebrew word for Spain, used to refer to those descended from the Jews of Spain and Portugal. Some Sephardic rituals, customs and religious observances differ from those of German or Eastern European — *Ashkenazic* — Jews. Sephardic pronunciation of Hebrew is different too, and is in fact the official pronunciation used in Israel. The Sephardim also developed a dialect of their own called America, including Brazil, Colombia, Argentina and Spanish words similar in concept though not in sound to Yiddish.

The Spanish Jews never really recovered, although today there are active communities in Malaga and other places, and 3,000 Jews live in Madrid. But sizeable Sephardic populations are found throughout Latin America, including Brazil, Columbia, Argentina and Mexico, and there are large communities in Mexico City, Buenos Aires and elsewhere. Traditional Jewish cooking in Spain, Portugal and Latin America tends to be quite

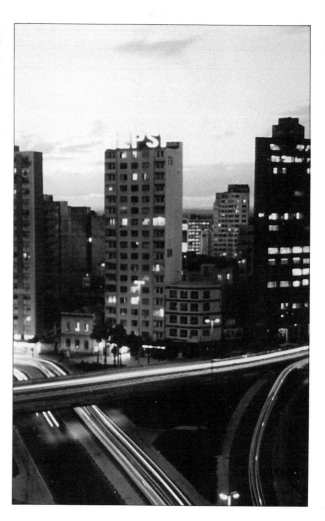

similar to the local cuisine, with modifications to take account of the kosher laws. The recipe for paella given here, for example, omits shellfish. The modern Jewish population of the Spanish- and Portuguese-speaking world also includes many who fled from Hitler, bringing with them cooking traditions from elsewhere in Europe. Although no really distinct Sephardic cuisine exists, the dishes given here provide a broad cross-section of Jewish cooking styles in Spain, Portugal and the New World.

Jewish cuisine from Spain, Portugal and Latin America makes wide use of colourful local ingredients and traditions.

Holiday Fried Chicken ABOVE (OPPOSITE) *(page 167).*

♦

Red Snapper Jewish-Style BELOW LEFT (OPPOSITE) *(page 170).*

♦

Stewed Fennel BELOW RIGHT (OPPOSITE) *(page 171).*

♦

Cinnamon Turnovers ABOVE *(page 173).*

♦

Stuffed Mushrooms Provençal BELOW *(page 156).*

Fisherman's Stew ABOVE *is a kosher adaptation of
the classic French dish, Bouillabaisse (page 159).*

♦

Chocolate Mousse BELOW *is an elaborate dessert
well worth the effort (page 161).*

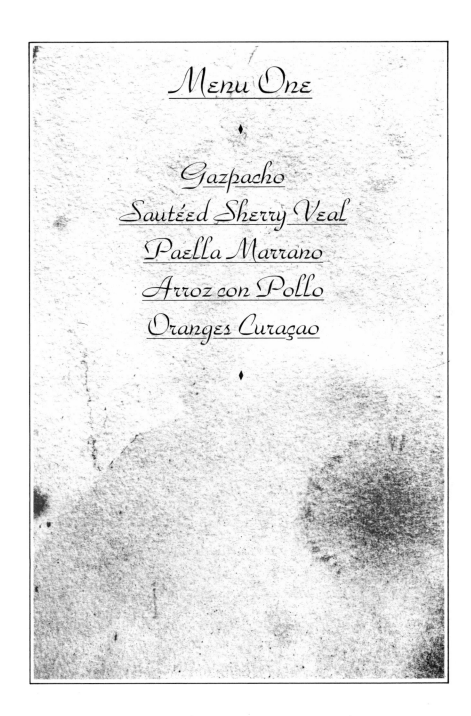

Menu One

♦

Gazpacho

Sautéed Sherry Veal

Paella Marrano

Arroz con Pollo

Oranges Curaçao

♦

Gazpacho

SERVES 6—8

This chilled vegetable soup is delightfully refreshing on hot days.

2 cucumbers, peeled and coarsely chopped

5 tomatoes, peeled, seeded and coarsely chopped

1 cup diced onion

1 green pepper, coarsely chopped

4 cups coarse unflavored breadcrumbs

3 garlic cloves, finely chopped

4 cups cold water

$\frac{1}{4}$ cup red wine vinegar

1 teaspoon salt

3 tablespoons olive oil

$1\frac{1}{2}$ tablespoons tomato paste

1 cup each chopped onion, green pepper and peeled cucumber for garnish

In a large wooden mixing bowl, combine all ingredients except the garnishes. Mix thoroughly and then beat with an eggbeater until fairly smooth. Cover the bowl tightly and chill for 2 to 3 hours.

◆ Sprinkle the chopped vegetables over the individual soup bowls and serve.

Sautéed Sherry Veal

SERVES 6

1 cup olive oil

1 cup green olives, pitted and halved

$\frac{1}{4}$ pound mushrooms, coarsely chopped

2 cups finely chopped onions

2 green peppers, seeded and finely chopped

4 garlic cloves, finely chopped

4 ripe tomatoes, peeled, seeded and finely chopped

3 pounds thin veal scallops

1 cup flour

$\frac{1}{4}$ teaspoon salt

$\frac{1}{4}$ teaspoon black pepper

$\frac{1}{2}$ cup dry sherry

$\frac{1}{2}$ cup water

Heat half of the olive oil in a large heavy skillet. Add the olives, mushrooms, onions, green pepper, garlic and tomatoes. Cook, stirring frequently, for 15 minutes over a low heat. Set aside.

◆ Dredge the veal scallops in a mixture of the flour, salt and pepper.

◆ In another skillet, heat the remaining olive oil over a low heat. Add the veal scallops, in batches if necessary, and cook for 3 to 4 minutes per side. As the scallops are cooked, set them aside in a warm place.

◆ Drain the oil and fat from the skillet. Add the sherry, water and cooked vegetables. Cover and simmer for 8 minutes over a medium heat. Pour the sauce over the veal and serve hot.

Paella Marrano

SERVES 8

In Spain there are literally hundreds of variations of this famous dish. This kosher version uses neither pork nor shellfish.

$\frac{1}{2}$ cup olive oil

1 pound spicy kosher beef sausage, sliced

$\frac{3}{4}$ pound cubed stewing veal

$\frac{3}{4}$ pound cubed stewing beef

2 pound chicken, cut into small pieces

1 pound striped bass fillets, cut into small pieces

1 pound red snapper fillets, cut into small pieces

1 pound salmon steak, cut into small pieces

1 pound haddock fillets, cut into small pieces

1 pound bluefish fillets, cut into small pieces

1 teaspoon salt

$\frac{1}{2}$ teaspoon black pepper

$\frac{1}{2}$ cup finely chopped onions

1 green pepper, seeded and finely chopped

1 large tomato, peeled, seeded and finely chopped

4 garlic cloves, finely chopped

3 cups rice

$\frac{1}{4}$ teaspoon saffron threads

6 cups boiling water

$\frac{1}{2}$ pound peas

In a medium-sized heavy skillet, heat 3 tablespoons of the olive oil. Add the sausage slices and brown well over a low heat. Remove the sausage slices and set aside.

♦ In the same skillet, heat another 2 tablespoons of the olive oil. Add the veal and beef cubes and brown well over a low heat. Cook for 10 minutes after the meats are browned. Remove from the skillet and set aside.

♦ In the same skillet, brown the chicken pieces over a moderate heat for 15 to 20 minutes, or until thoroughly cooked. Remove the pieces and set aside.

♦ Drain the fat from the skillet. Add 4 tablespoons of the olive oil and heat over a low heat. Add the fish pieces, salt, pepper, onions, green pepper, tomatoes and garlic. Sauté for 15 to 20 minutes or until the fish are cooked but still firm. Set aside.

♦ Preheat the oven to 400°F. In a large paella pan or flameproof casserole combine the sautéed fish and vegetables with the rice, saffron and boiling water. Stir well and bring to a boil over a high heat. Remove the pan from the heat.

♦ Arrange the pieces of sausage, chicken, veal and beef and the peas over the rice mixture. Bake, uncovered, for 30 minutes, or until all the liquid is absorbed.

♦ Remove the pan from the oven and cover with a clean tea-towel. Leave it to stand for 5 minutes. Serve with lemon wedges for garnish.

Arroz con Pollo

SERVES 8

Rice with chicken is a classic Spanish meal, hearty and easy to prepare. Serve it with a simple salad, a glass of wine and a simple dessert.

2 tablespoons chicken fat
2 × 3 pound chickens, cut into serving pieces
$\frac{1}{4}$ teaspoon salt
$\frac{1}{4}$ teaspoon black pepper
2 cups finely chopped onion
4 garlic cloves, finely chopped
$1\frac{1}{2}$ tablespoons sweet paprika
4 ripe tomatoes, skinned, seeded and finely chopped
2 cups peas
$\frac{1}{2}$ teaspoon crumbled saffron threads
3 tablespoons finely chopped parsley
3 cups rice
6 cups boiling water

Melt the chicken fat in a large paella pan or saucepan. Add the chicken pieces, salt and pepper and cook over a moderate heat for 40 minutes. Turn the chicken pieces frequently.

♦ Remove the chicken pieces from the pan and set them aside.

♦ Add the onions, garlic, paprika, tomatoes, peas, saffron and parsley to the pan. Cook over a low heat for 10 minutes, stirring frequently.

♦ Return the chicken to the pan. Add the rice and boiling water. Stir well and bring to a boil over a high heat. Reduce the heat to low. Cover the pan and simmer for 40 minutes. Remove the pan from the heat. Remove the lid and leave it to stand for 5 minutes before serving.

Oranges Curaçao

SERVES 4

The first synagogue in the New World was built on Curaçao in the early sixteenth century by Sephardic Jews.

2 large navel oranges, peeled
4 teaspoons brown sugar
4 tablespoons Curaçao or other orange-flavoured liqueur

Cut each orange into $\frac{1}{8}$ inch thick slices and quarter each slice into wedge shapes. Arrange the orange wedges on individual serving plates. Sprinkle each plate with 1 teaspoon of the brown sugar and 1 tablespoon of the Curaçao. Chill for 30 minutes or until ready to serve.

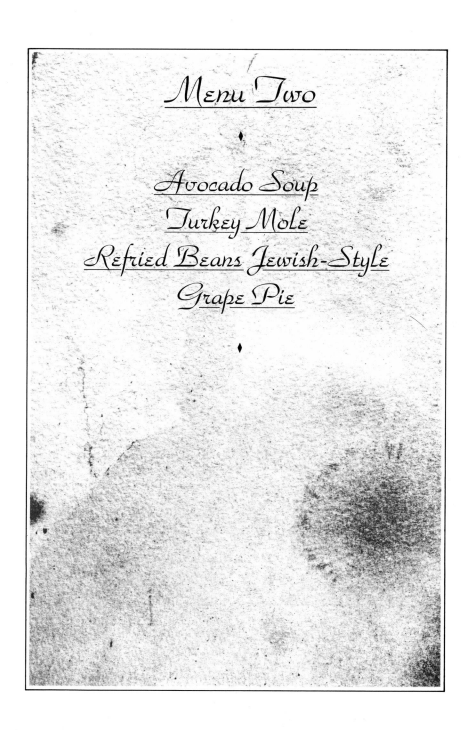

Menu Two

♦

Avocado Soup
Turkey Mole
Refried Beans Jewish-Style
Grape Pie

♦

Avocado Soup

SERVES 6

Avocado soup is easy to make and provides an authentic Mexican start to a meal.

3 large avocados, peeled and mashed
2 tablespoons lemon juice
$\frac{1}{2}$ teaspoon salt
$\frac{1}{4}$ teaspoon black pepper
$\frac{1}{4}$ teaspoon grated nutmeg
$\frac{1}{4}$ teaspoon cayenne pepper
6 cups chicken broth

Combine all the ingredients except the chicken broth in a small mixing bowl. Mash to a smooth paste.

♦ In a medium-sized saucepan, heat the chicken broth over a low heat. Gradually stir in the avocado paste. Stir until the mixture is smooth and even. Bring to a boil and serve hot.

Turkey Mole

SERVES 8

The literal translation of the name of this recipe is turkey in chocolate sauce — which may sound a little odd! In fact, this authentic Mexican dish uses unsweetened chocolate and has a rich, cinnamon taste that is quite unusual.

8-10 pound turkey, cut into 8 serving pieces
2 cups finely chopped onions
3 tomatoes, skinned, seeded and coarsely chopped
$\frac{1}{2}$ cup chopped golden seedless raisins
$\frac{1}{2}$ teaspoon ground coriander
1 teaspoon cayenne pepper
2 garlic cloves, finely chopped
$\frac{1}{2}$ teaspoon ground cinnamon
$\frac{1}{2}$ teaspoon ground cloves
$\frac{3}{4}$ cup finely chopped almonds
$\frac{1}{2}$ teaspoon salt
$\frac{1}{4}$ teaspoon black pepper
2 cups boiling chicken broth
4 tablespoons chicken fat
2 cups cold chicken broth
$1\frac{1}{2}$ ounces unsweetened chocolate

Place the turkey pieces in a large saucepan and cover with water. Cover the pan and cook over a high heat for 15 minutes. Reduce the heat to medium and cook for a further 45 minutes.

♦ Meanwhile, combine the onions, tomatoes, raisins, coriander, cayenne pepper, garlic, cinnamon, cloves, almonds, salt, pepper and boiling chicken broth in a large wooden mixing bowl. Mix to a paste.

♦ In a large skillet, melt the chicken fat over a low heat. Add the chopped vegetables and spice mixture. Fry for 5 minutes, stirring constantly.

♦ Add the cold chicken broth and chocolate to the skillet. Cook for 10 to 12 minutes over a moderate heat, or until the chocolate has completely melted. Stir constantly until the chocolate is evenly distributed throughout the mole sauce.
♦ Preheat the oven to 450°F. Remove the turkey pieces from the skillet and drain well. Pat the pieces dry with paper towels. Arrange the turkey pieces in a large baking dish in a single layer. Bake, uncovered, for 30 minutes.
♦ Pour the sauce over the turkey pieces and lower the heat to 350°F. Cook for a further 30 minutes. You can sprinkle the dish with sesame seeds before serving.

Refried Beans Jewish-style

SERVES 6

This Jewish version of the famous Mexican peasant recipe can be served as a side dish.

1 cup chicken fat
½ cup finely chopped onion
½ cup finely chopped green pepper
3 garlic cloves, finely chopped
1 teaspoon salt
1 teaspoon chili powder
5 cups cooked pinto beans, drained

Melt the chicken fat in a large heavy skillet. Add the onion, pepper, garlic, salt and chili powder and sauté over a medium heat for 8 to 10 minutes. Add the beans and sauté for a further 10 minutes, stirring occasionally. Serve hot.

Grape Pie

MAKES 1 PIE

This Central American pie has a flavor similar to blueberry pie, but is not as heavy.

2 quarts Concord grapes
½ cup sugar
½ tablespoon cornstarch
¼ cup Triple Sec liqueur
1 tablespoon melted butter
8 ounces singlecrust pastry

Preheat the oven to 450°F. Peel the grapes, set the skin aside and discard the pips. In a large saucepan, mash the grapes to a pulp and bring them to a boil over a low heat.
♦ Strain the pulp through a fine sieve into another saucepan. Discard any solids remaining in the sieve.
♦ Add the reserved grape skins, sugar, cornstarch, liqueur and butter to the pulp. Stir well and heat gently over a low heat for 3 to 5 minutes, or until the pulp is warm but not hot.
♦ Line a 9 inch pie dish with half the pastry. Fill the pie shell with the grape pulp. Roll out the remaining pastry and cover the pie, sealing the edges carefully. Cut steam vents into the top crust.
♦ Bake for 15 minutes. Reduce the oven temperature to 375°F and bake for a further 40 minutes. Allow to cool before serving.

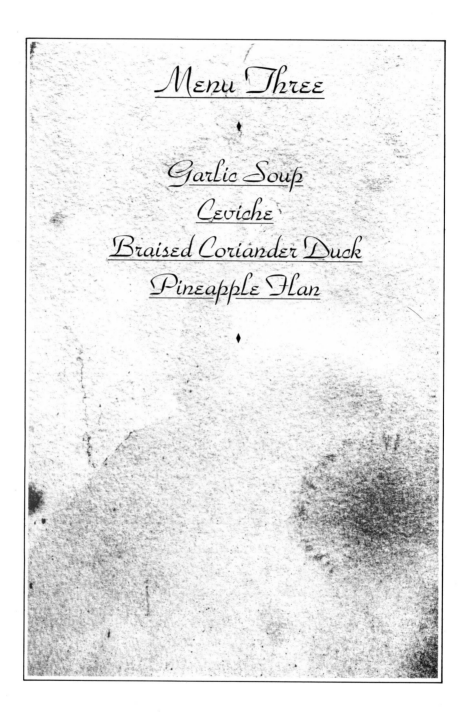

Menu Three

◆

Garlic Soup
Ceviche
Braised Coriander Duck
Pineapple Flan

◆

Garlic Soup

SERVES 6—8

Variations of this rich and tasty soup are found throughout the Spanish-speaking world.

$\frac{1}{2}$ cup olive oil
8 garlic cloves
1 teaspoon paprika
$\frac{1}{8}$ teaspoon cayenne pepper
6 slices stale white bread, cubed
$7\frac{1}{2}$ cups boiling water
2 teaspoons salt
1 teaspoon freshly ground black pepper
6 eggs, beaten

Heat the olive oil in a large heavy saucepan. Add the garlic and sauté until the cloves are golden brown. Stir in the paprika and cayenne pepper. Add the bread cubes and sauté until they are firm and golden. Carefully add the boiling water to the pan, making sure the fried bread cubes are not broken. Add the salt and pepper. Cover the pan and simmer for 1 hour.

♦ Slowly pour the beaten eggs into the pan, stirring constantly. Simmer until the eggs are firm. Serve at once.

Ceviche

SERVES 6

This dish can be traced back to the Peruvian Incas. The fish 'cooks' in the lime juice.

1 cup fresh lime juice
1 cup fresh lemon juice
4 dried red chili peppers, finely ground
2 large Spanish or red onions, thinly sliced
2 garlic cloves, finely chopped
1 teaspoon salt
$\frac{1}{4}$ teaspoon black pepper
$2\frac{1}{2}$ pounds sole or flounder fillets, cut into 1 inch square pieces
1 large head of lettuce

In a large glass or ceramic dish, combine the lime juice, lemon juice, ground chili peppers, onions, garlic, salt and pepper. Stir well. Add the fish pieces and submerge then in the marinade.

♦ Cover and chill for 4 hours. Serve cold on a bed of lettuce.

Braised Coriander Duck

SERVES 6

The origins of this dish are hard to trace. It is served in South America, but seems to have a touch of Arab influence.

5-6 pound duck, cut into 6 serving pieces and trimmed of fat

$\frac{1}{4}$ cup lemon juice

$\frac{1}{2}$ teaspoon ground cumin

$\frac{1}{2}$ teaspoon salt

$\frac{1}{2}$ teaspoon black pepper

$\frac{1}{4}$ cup olive oil

32 ounces light beer

2 cups rice

1 cup cooked peas

1 cup finely chopped fresh coriander leaves

Brush the duck with a mixture of the lemon juice, cumin, salt and pepper. Place on a plate, cover and refrigerate for 4 to 5 hours.

♦ In a large flameproof casserole, heat the olive oil over a medium heat. Add the duck pieces and brown them on all sides. Pour off all but 1 tablespoon of the fat.

♦ Add the beer to the casserole and bring to a boil. Cover and reduce the heat to low. Simmer for 50 minutes.

♦ Remove the duck pieces from the casserole. Set them aside and keep warm.

♦

♦ Remove 3 cups of the liquid from the casserole and bring it to a boil in a medium-sized saucepan over a high heat. Add the rice, stir, bring to a boil again and cover tightly. Reduce the heat to low and simmer for 18 minutes.

♦ Stir the peas and coriander leaves into the rice. Cover, remove from the heat and allow to stand for 1 minute. Arrange the duck pieces on a bed of rice and serve.

Pineapple Flan

SERVES 6—8

Popular throughout Mexico and South America, this dish has its origins in Spain.

$1\frac{1}{4}$ cups sugar

$\frac{1}{2}$ cup water

3 eggs plus 2 egg yolks

15 ounce can condensed milk

$1\frac{1}{2}$ cups pineapple juice

In a small saucepan, bring 1 cup of the sugar and the water to a boil over a high heat. Reduce the heat to medium and stir gently. Boil for 10 to 15 minutes, or until the caramel turns a dark golden brown.

♦ Remove the saucepan from the heat and pour the caramel along the sides of a 6 cup porcelain mold, tilting the mold back and forth to get a thin, even coating. When the caramel begins to set, turn the mold upside-down over a sheet of waxed paper and leave it to cool for 2 minutes.

♦ Preheat the oven to 325°F. In a large mixing bowl, combine the eggs, egg yolks, condensed milk, remaining sugar and pineapple juice. Beat until the consistency of the mixture is even throughout. Pour the mixture into the caramel-lined mold. Place the mold inside a baking dish half-filled with boiling water. Bake for 1 hour. Chill the mold for at least 3 hours.

♦ To serve, invert the mold over a dish and remove the flan by running a butter knife carefully around the edges of the mold. Serve cold.

Ceviche ABOVE *is a Jewish adaptation of an*
ancient Peruvian dish (page 189).

♦

Paella Marrano BELOW *is a kosher version of one*
of the most famous Spanish dishes of all
(page 183).

The English Speaking World

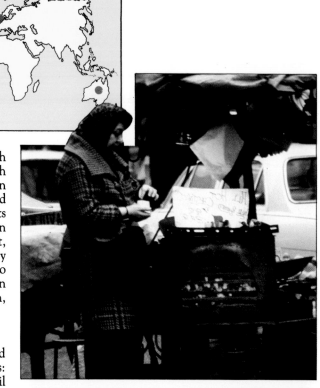

Britain Although there were already Jews in Britain, the expulsion of the Jews from Spain in the fifteenth century brought them in shiploads to the comparatively tolerant British shores. Queen Elizabeth I had a Jewish physician, and later, in the eighteenth and nineteenth centuries, many Jews rose to considerable prominence in British society. The British branch of the Rothschild banking house was highly successful, and one of its members was admitted to the House of Lords, while in 1874 Benjamin Disraeli, who was of Jewish descent, became Prime Minister. In the late nineteenth century thousands of Russian Jews fleeing Tsarist persecution also came to Britain, and today the British Jewish population numbers half a million, living mostly in London, Manchester, Birmingham and Glasgow.

The United States In 1954 American Jews celebrated three hundred years of settlement in the United States: the first Jewish settlers had arrived in New York from Brazil in 1654. One of the oldest Jewish cemeteries in America, founded in 1677, is in Newport, Rhode Island, as is the famous Touro Synagogue, which dates from 1763. From the beginning of the eighteenth century to the present day, North America has been a haven for Jews from all over the world. German emigrants arrived during the fifty years from 1820 to 1870, while a much larger influx of Eastern European Jews began in 1881 and continued until the outbreak of World War I. Today, there are over six million Jews in the United States. For decades the major port of entry was New York City, where emigrants were symbolically welcomed by the Statue of Liberty and officially processed on Ellis Island. Others arrived via Boston, Philadelphia, Baltimore and Montreal, and in the crowded tenements of New York's Lower East Side and elsewhere, they established vital, thriving communities. Yiddish theatre, Yiddish newspapers, synagogues, social organizations and schools all flourished in the unaccustomed freedom enjoyed by the Jews in North America.

Because the major waves of Russian and Eastern European migration have had such a profound effect on Jewish culture in Britain and the United States, people tend to think of their cooking as 'Jewish cooking'. And in America, of course, such 'Jewish' foods as kosher hot dogs and bagels have become part of the standard urban cuisine. The Jewish populations of both countries, however, have a wide range of origins, and their cooking has also been deeply influenced by the culinary styles of their adopted homes. For these reasons, no truly distinct British or American Jewish cuisine has emerged, and it is not really possible to present a typical British or American Jewish menu. Instead this section presents a number of favorite dishes from both Britain and the United States organized in suggested menus.

The Jews of the English-Speaking World came from all over the globe. Diverse cooking styles met here and merged to form a unique cuisine.

Sweet and Sour Salmon ABOVE *is a piquant dish
that makes an excellent first course (page 204).*

◆

Lox and Onions Omelette BELOW *served with
bagels makes a perfect light lunch (page 205).*

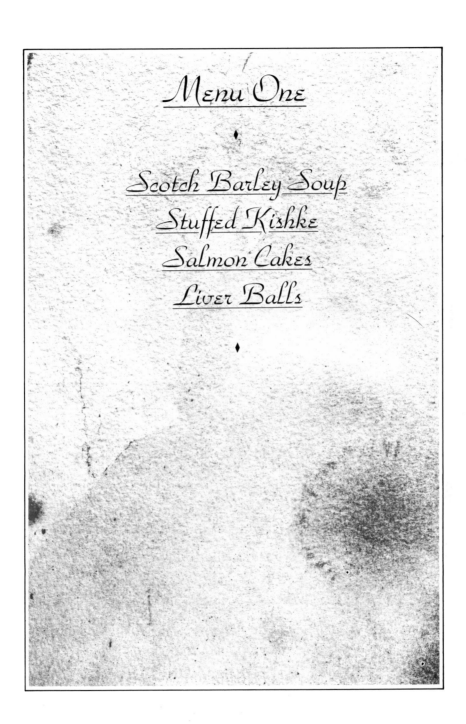

Menu One

♦

Scotch Barley Soup
Stuffed Kishke
Salmon Cakes
Liver Balls

♦

Scotch Barley Soup

SERVES 8

Glasgow has a large Jewish population. This dish is a variation of the popular Scottish dish.

6 tablespoons butter or margarine
6 carrots, grated
3 onions, coarsely chopped
2 turnips, cubed
3 quarts water
$1\frac{1}{2}$ cups pearl barley
1 teaspoon salt
black pepper to taste
chopped parsley

Melt the butter or margarine in a large saucepan. Add the carrots, onions and turnips and sauté for 5 minutes. Add the water and bring to a boil.
♦ Add the barley, salt and pepper. Cook over a low heat for 2 hours. Stir in the parsley and serve.

Stuffed Kishke

SERVES 8

Probably of Eastern European origin, the recipe here is a British version of this famous dish. Serve slices of the kishke as a starter or as a side dish with meat or poultry.

3 feet kosher beef sausage casing
1 cup sifted flour
$\frac{1}{2}$ cup matzoh meal
$\frac{1}{4}$ cup grated onion
$1\frac{1}{2}$ teaspoons salt
$\frac{1}{4}$ teaspoon black pepper
1 teaspoon paprika
1 cup chicken fat
2 onions, sliced

Rinse the inside and outside of the casing. Cut the casing in half. Tie up one end of each half.
♦ Mix the flour, matzoh meal, grated onion, salt, pepper, paprika and $\frac{3}{4}$ cup of the chicken fat in a large bowl. Stuff the casings with the mixture and tie up the open ends. Cook the kishke in a large saucepan of boiling water for 1 hour. Drain well.
♦ Preheat the oven to 350°F.
♦ Spread the remaining fat in a baking dish. Arrange the onion slices in the dish. Place the kishke in the dish and bake for $1\frac{1}{2}$ hours, basting frequently with the pan drippings.

Salmon Cakes

SERVES 8

Strange as it sounds today, salmon was once a cheap fish, the food of the poor.

> 3 pounds canned salmon, drained
>
> 1 teaspoon salt
>
> black pepper to taste
>
> 1 cup chopped onion
>
> $\frac{1}{2}$ cup butter or margarine, softened
>
> $\frac{1}{2}$ cup flour
>
> $\frac{1}{2}$ cup heavy cream
>
> $\frac{3}{4}$ cup vegetable oil

Chop the salmon very finely in a mixing bowl. Add the salt and pepper. Add the onions, butter, flour and cream and mix until smooth. Shape the mixture into balls or cakes.

♦ Heat the vegetable oil in a large heavy skillet. Add the salmon cakes and sauté until golden brown on both sides.

Liver Balls

SERVES 8

This is a delicious variation on chopped liver, one of the classic dishes of Jewish cuisine.

> 2 tablespoons chicken fat
>
> 2 tablespoons chopped onion
>
> $\frac{1}{2}$ pound fresh chicken livers, chopped
>
> 1 egg yolk
>
> $1\frac{1}{2}$ tablespoons potato flour
>
> $\frac{1}{2}$ teaspoon salt
>
> black pepper to taste
>
> 1 egg white, stiffly beaten

Melt the chicken fat in a large skillet. Add the chopped onions and sauté until lightly browned. Add the chopped livers to the onions and sauté until browned.

♦ Remove the skillet from the heat and stir in the egg yolk, potato flour, salt and pepper. Fold in the egg white.

♦ Bring a large pan of salted water to a boil. Drop teaspoonfuls of the liver mixture into the boiling water until all the mixture is used up. Cook until the balls rise to the surface. Remove, drain well and serve.

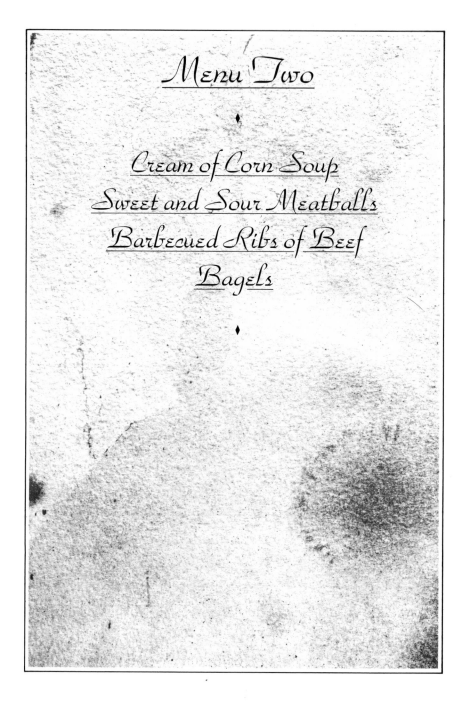

Menu Two

♦

Cream of Corn Soup
Sweet and Sour Meatballs
Barbecued Ribs of Beef
Bagels

♦

Cream of Corn Soup

SERVES 8

This classic American soup has gradually found its way into Jewish kitchens.

> 4 tablespoons butter or margarine
>
> $\frac{1}{4}$ cup finely chopped onion
>
> 2 tablespoons flour
>
> 4 cups milk
>
> 2 cups cooked corn
>
> 1 teaspoon salt
>
> black pepper to taste

Melt the butter in a saucepan. Add the onions and sauté for 3 minutes. Stir in the flour and milk. Slowly bring the mixture to a boil and add the corn, salt and pepper. Cook over a low heat for 15 minutes.

Sweet and Sour Meatballs

SERVES 6

This dish is excellent for buffets, and also freezes well.

> $1\frac{1}{2}$ pounds lean ground beef
>
> 3 tablespoons grated onion
>
> 1 egg
>
> 1 teaspoon salt
>
> black pepper to taste
>
> 2 tablespoons cornstarch
>
> 2 tablespoons margarine
>
> $1\frac{1}{2}$ tablespoons lemon juice
>
> $1\frac{1}{2}$ cups beef broth
>
> $\frac{1}{4}$ cup seedless raisins
>
> 1 lemon, thinly sliced
>
> 2 tablespoons honey
>
> 6 ginger snaps, crushed

Combine the meat, onion, egg, salt and pepper in a mixing bowl. Shape the mixture into 1 inch balls. Roll the balls lightly in the cornstarch.
♦ Melt the margarine in a deep skillet. Add the meatballs and brown on all sides. Add the lemon juice, broth, raisins, lemon and honey. Cover and cook over a low heat for 35 minutes. Stir the crushed ginger snaps into the sauce. Cook for a further 10 minutes.

Barbecued Ribs of Beef

SERVES 6—8

Barbecued dishes in general are enjoying a resurgence of popularity in America.

3 pounds beef short ribs, cut into 2 inch pieces
1 tablespoon vegetable oil
1 teaspoon salt
$\frac{1}{4}$ teaspoon pepper
1 teaspoon paprika
1 teaspoon dry mustard
1 tablespoon sugar
1 tablespoon Worcestershire sauce
$\frac{1}{2}$ cup tomato ketchup
$\frac{1}{2}$ cup water
$\frac{1}{4}$ cup cider vinegar
$\frac{1}{2}$ cup finely chopped onion
1 garlic clove, finely chopped

Preheat the oven to 350°F. Heat the vegetable oil in a flameproof casserole. Add the rib pieces and brown on all sides. Pour off the fat. Add the remaining ingredients to the casserole. Cover and bake for 2 hours. Remove the cover for the last 30 minutes. Arrange on a dish with parsley and serve.

Austrian Bagels

MAKES 12 BAGELS

Historians of the bagel recount that in 1683 an anonymous Viennese baker decided to honor the King of Poland's favorite pastime, riding, by making a bread roll in the shape of a stirrup. The German word for stirrup is buegel *— hence the modern* bagel. *The controversy over what makes a proper bagel continues to rage. But there is no dispute that the true bagel is boiled first and then baked, giving it a dense texture.*

1 package active dry yeast
$1\frac{1}{2}$ cups warm water
2 tablespoons sugar
$\frac{1}{2}$ teaspoon salt
$4\frac{1}{4}$ cups flour
4 quarts water

Dissolve the yeast in the warm water in a large bowl. Add the sugar, salt and flour and stir to form a soft dough.
♦ Turn the dough out on to a floured surface and knead until smooth and elastic, about 10 minutes. Cover the dough with a tea-towel and leave to rise for 15 minutes.
♦ Flatten the dough and roll out to a thickness of 1 inch. Cut the dough into strips 12 inches long and 1 inch wide. Roll each strip into a cylinder with a diameter of $\frac{1}{2}$ inch. Cut each cylinder in half. Pinch together the ends of the strips to form circles.
♦ Cover the bagels with a tea-towel and leave them to rise for 20 minutes.
♦ Bring the water to a boil in a large pot. Preheat the oven to 375°F.
♦ Add the bagels in batches of 4 to the boiling water, reduce the heat, and simmer for 7 minutes. Remove the bagels, drain well, and place them on baking sheets. Bake for 30 minutes.

Menu Three

♦

Sweet and Sour Salmon
Vegetable Cutlets
Lox and Onions Omelette
Lemon Cheesecake

♦

Sweet and Sour Salmon

SERVES 8

A light and piquant dish that makes an excellent appetizer to a dairy meal.

3 onions, sliced

3 lemons, sliced

½ cup honey

⅓ cup seedless raisins

1 bay leaf

8 thin salmon steaks

1 teaspoon salt

3 cups water

8 crushed ginger snaps

½ cup cider vinegar

½ cup sliced blanched almonds

Combine the onions, lemon slices, honey, raisins, bay leaf, salmon steaks, salt and water in a large saucepan. Cover and cook over a low heat for 30 minutes. Remove the fish.

♦ Add the ginger snaps, vinegar and almonds to the fish stock. Cook over a low heat. Stir until smooth. Pour over the fish, and serve either warm or cold.

Vegetable Cutlets

SERVES 6

Kosher dairy restaurants are common in the Jewish areas of large American cities such as New York and Baltimore. This substantial dish is often featured on the menu.

2 tablespoons butter

1 cup chopped onion

½ cup chopped celery

1 cup grated carrots

½ cup coarsely chopped cooked green beans

½ cup cooked peas

3 eggs

1 teaspoon salt

½ teaspoon black pepper

3 tablespoons matzoh meal

vegetable oil

Melt the butter in a skillet. Add the onion, celery and carrots and sauté for 10 minutes. Remove from the heat. Add the green beans, peas, 2 of the eggs, and the salt, pepper and matzoh meal. Mix well. Shape the mixture into 6 cutlets.

♦ Beat the remaining egg in a bowl. Dip the cutlets into the egg.

♦ Heat the vegetable oil in a skillet. Add the cutlets and sauté until both sides are browned.

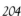

Lox and Onions Omelette

SERVES 4

Lox is the Yiddish name for smoked salmon, and this recipe makes a perfect meal for a light lunch. Serve it with bagels in authentic Jewish style.

> 8 eggs
>
> $\frac{1}{2}$ pound lox or Nova Scotia smoked salmon, cubed
>
> 1 onion, finely chopped
>
> black pepper to taste
>
> 4 teaspoons butter

Beat the eggs in a bowl. Stir in the salmon, onion and pepper.

♦ Melt 1 teaspoon of the butter in a skillet. Add a quarter of the egg mixture and cook over a low heat until the omelette is solid. Repeat with the remaining egg mixture, making four omelettes in all.

Lemon Cheesecake

MAKES 1 10 INCH CAKE

> 4 cups graham cracker crumbs
>
> 1 cup sweet butter, melted
>
> $1\frac{1}{2}$ tablespoons unflavored gelatin
>
> $\frac{1}{4}$ cup cold water
>
> $\frac{3}{4}$ cup sugar
>
> 5 large eggs, separated
>
> pinch of salt
>
> $\frac{1}{3}$ cup milk, scalded
>
> 24 ounces cream cheese, softened
>
> $\frac{1}{3}$ cup lemon juice
>
> $\frac{1}{4}$ cup orange-flavored liqueur
>
> $\frac{1}{2}$ teaspoon pure vanilla extract
>
> finely grated rind of 2 lemons

Preheat the oven to 350°F. In a large bowl combine the graham cracker crumbs and melted butter. Mix well. Remove $\frac{1}{3}$ cup of the crumbs and set aside. Press the remaining crumbs into the bottom and up the sides of a buttered 10 inch deep cake pan with spring clip. Bake for 12 to 15 minutes or until firm. Remove from the oven and cool on a wire rack.

♦ In a small cup, soften the gelatin in the cold water for 4 to 5 minutes.

♦ In the top part of a double boiler, combine $\frac{3}{4}$ cup of the sugar, the egg yolks and salt. Beat well. Place over slowly simmering water. Add the scalded milk, a little at a time, beating constantly for about 5 minutes, until it is thick and smooth. Add the gelatin mixture and stir until dissolved. Remove from the heat and cool.

♦ In a large bowl beat the cream cheese until smooth. Add a small amount of the egg yolk mixture and beat well. Fold in the remaining egg yolk mixture. Add the lemon juice, orange liqueur and vanilla extract. Fold in until well blended.

♦ In a large bowl beat the egg whites until soft peaks begin to form. Add the remaining $\frac{1}{2}$ cup of sugar, a little at a time, beating until stiff but not dry. Gently fold the egg whites into the cheese mixture.

♦ Turn the mixture into the prepared pan. Smooth with a rubber spatula and sprinkle with the reserved crumbs and the grated lemon rind. Refrigerate for 8 hours.

Holiday Recipes

Nineteenth-century ceremonial towel used at the
seder during the festival of Passover.

Blintzes ABOVE LEFT are a traditional Shavuot dish
(page 211).

◆

Hamentaschen ABOVE RIGHT are served at Purim,
either with a prune filling or a poppy-seed filling
(page 215).

◆

Potato Pancakes BELOW are a classic of Jewish
cuisine around the world and are traditionally
served at Chanuka (page 217).

Sabbath

At the beginning of the Bible we are told that God rested on the seventh day. The Sabbath — a holy day of rest, prayer and study — is one of the foundations of the Jewish faith.

The Sabbath, or Shabbos, is ushered in at sundown on Friday evening when the women of the household light and bless the Sabbath candles. After attendance at services, kiddush, the benediction over the wine, is recited and a Sabbath meal is served. Songs of praise, zemirot, are sung. On Saturday, the week's portion of the Torah is read at the synagogue. The day is devoted to rest and study. Shabbos ends at sundown on Saturday evening with the beautiful havdalah ceremony, where blessings are recited over wine, spices and a braided candle.

Because no fires can be lit or work done on the Sabbath, the foods served onSaturday are often either prepared the day before or cooked slowly over a very low heat starting late on Friday afternoon. Dishes which can be served hot or cold, such as kugels, are favorite Sabbath dishes.

In poorer households before World War II, the Sabbath was often the only time meat was served. A simple roast chicken is a traditional Friday night meal. Cholent, a slowly baked casserole of beans and meat, is traditional on Saturday among Eastern European Jews. Challah, braided egg bread, is virtually obligatory on the Sabbath whatever country you are in, as is red grape wine for the kiddush.

Petcha

SERVES 8

This traditional European Sabbath dish is often served at lunch. It can be made several days in advance.

$2\frac{1}{2}$ pounds calves' feet

4 garlic cloves

1 tablespoon salt

black pepper to taste

sliced lemons, oranges or radishes to garnish

Clean and chop the calves' feet. Place them in a saucepan and cover completely with cold water. Add the garlic, salt and pepper. Bring the water to a boil, then cover and simmer for 5 hours.

♦ Remove the feet from the liquid. Remove the meat from the bones. Discard the bones and mince the meat. Return the meat to the liquid and boil for 5 minutes.

♦ Pour the mixture into a dish and leave it to cool. Cover the dish tightly with plastic wrap or aluminum foil and refrigerate for several hours, or until the liquid has become gelatinous and firm. Remove any fat with a paper towel. Cut into wedges and serve garnished with sliced lemons, oranges or radishes.

Lokschen Kugel

SERVES 8

Kugel is a traditional Sabbath dinner dish, but can be enjoyed any time, served either hot or at room temperature.

4 tablespoons melted margarine

$\frac{1}{2}$ pound thick egg noodles

salt

2 eggs

$\frac{1}{3}$ cup honey

2 large cooking apples, peeled, cored and grated

2 tablespoons lemon juice

$\frac{1}{2}$ cup seedless raisins

$\frac{1}{2}$ cup chopped walnuts

Preheat the oven to 375°F. Grease a flameproof casserole with one tablespoon of the margarine.

♦ Cook the noodles in a large pan of salted boiling water until they are just *al dente*, about 5 minutes. Drain, rinse with cold water, and drain well again.

♦ In a large bowl beat the eggs and add the honey. Add the apples, lemon juice, noodles, raisins, walnuts and remaining margarine. Mix gently but well. Pour the mixture into the casserole.

♦ Bake until the top is golden brown, about 1 hour.

שבועות
Shavuot

Also called Pentecost, the Feast of Weeks, or the Festival of the First
Fruits, Shavuot is a harvest festival. It also celebrates the giving of the
Ten Commandments to Moses on Mount Sinai.
Shavuot begins on the fiftieth day after the counting of the omer. A
sheaf of barley, the omer, was presented as a sacrifice on the second day
of Passover. Fifty days after that, on the sixth of Sivan, in May or June,
the first fruits of the harvest were offered. Since the wheat crop was
harvested at that time, the sacrifice consisted of wheat bread.
Because Shavuot is an agricultural holiday, it is customary to serve
wheat bread and dairy dishes, and to decorate the home with flowers.

בלינצ׳ס
Blintzes

SERVES 12

Today blintzes are served not only on Shavuot but as a Sunday brunch treat as well.

4 eggs
7 tablespoons flour
$\frac{1}{2}$ teaspoon salt
1 cup cold water
sweet butter
For the filling:
1 pound farmer cheese
6 ounces cream cheese
2 egg yolks
1 teaspoon pure vanilla extract
grated rind of 2 lemons
4 tablespoons sugar

Combine the eggs, flour, salt and water in a mixing bowl until very smooth. Cover
the bowl and refrigerate for several hours.
♦ Bring the batter back to room temperature. Mix again until it is very smooth.
♦ Melt the butter in a skillet over a medium heat. Add a drop of batter to the skillet.
When it sizzles, the butter is hot enough. Lift the skillet off the heat and drop 2
tablespoons of the batter into it. Swirl the batter around to coat the bottom of the
skillet thinly and evenly. Pour off any excess batter. Cook the blintz until lightly
browned on the bottom, then turn and cook on the other side until lightly
browned. Repeat until all the batter is used.
♦ To make the filling, blend the farmer cheese, cream cheese, egg yolks, vanilla,
lemon rind and sugar in a mixing bowl.
♦ Lay a blintz flat on a floured surface. Place 2 tablespoons of the filling on the
bottom half of the blintz. Roll up the blintz, tucking in the sides, into a rectangular,
tube-like package.
♦ Melt some additional butter in the skillet and add the blintzes. Cook on both sides
until golden.

Cheese Kugel

SERVES 8

This sweet noodle dish is also served on the Sabbath. Serve it hot, chilled or at room temperature.

$\frac{1}{2}$ pound medium egg noodles
1 tablespoon melted butter
1 pound farmer cheese
$\frac{1}{2}$ cup sugar
$\frac{1}{2}$ cup milk
$\frac{1}{2}$ cup orange juice
$\frac{1}{2}$ cup raisins
grated rind of 1 orange
2 eggs, separated

Preheat the oven to 375°F. Cook the noodles in a large pan of boiling salted water until they are *al dente*, about 5 minutes. Drain and rinse. Drain well.
♦ Mix the butter, farmer cheese, sugar, milk, orange juice, raisins, orange rind and egg yolks together in a large mixing bowl. Add the noodles and mix well.
♦ Beat the egg whites until they are stiff. Fold the egg whites into the noodle mixture. Fill a large greased baking dish with the mixture and bake for 20 minutes. Reduce the heat to 325°F and bake for a further 55 minutes.

Russian Pirogen

SERVES 6—8

The filling for Russian Pirogen is generally farmer cheese or curd cheese seasoned with sugar and cinnamon or with onions, salt and pepper. In either case, these simple dumplings should be served topped with lots of soured cream.

1 cup flour
1 teaspoon salt
1 cup potatoes, cooked, peeled and grated
1 egg
2 tablespoons water
$\frac{1}{2}$ cup butter
For the filling:
curd cheese
sugar and cinnamon or chopped onion, salt and pepper to taste

In a mixing bowl combine the flour and salt. Add the grated potatoes and mix well.
♦ In a small bowl, beat the egg and water together. Make a well in the flour mixture and pour the egg mixture into it. Mix well. Turn the dough out on to a floured surface and knead well. Roll the dough out to a thickness of $\frac{1}{4}$ inch. Cut the dough into 3 inch circles. Mix the sweet or savory filling. Put a spoonful of filling on to each circle and fold the dough over into a semicircular shape. Seal well, moistening the edges with a little water.
♦ Cook the pirogen in a large pan of boiling water for 5 minutes. Drain well.
♦ Melt the butter in a large skillet. Add the pirogen and fry until golden brown on both sides.

Passover

Passover falls on the fifteenth of Nisan, in March or April. This most ancient of Jewish holidays celebrates the deliverance of the Hebrews from slavery in Egypt some six thousand years ago.

The Hebrews left Egypt in such haste that the bread they were baking had no time to leaven. During Passover, observant Jews eat only matzoh and other unleavened foods. All the everyday kitchen utensils and eating implements are removed and special sets used only during Passover are brought out for the eight-day holiday.

The first and second nights of Passover are celebrated at the seder, a ritual where the story of Passover is retold and a substantial meal is served, followed by Passover songs and songs of praise. Four cups of wine are traditionally drunk at the seder.

The matzoh plate and the seder plate are prominent on the table. The plate holds three matzohs, the symbol of Passover. In the course of the ceremony, the middle matzoh is broken and half set aside for the afikomen, or dessert. Perhaps as a device to keep small children interested, it is traditional for someone to attempt to steal the afikomen and then ransom it back so that the seder can end.

The seder plate contains several symbolic items that are referred to during the ceremony. These include charoses, symbolizing the bricks used to build the pyramids; maror (bitter herbs) symbolizing the bitterness of slavery; parsley, symbolizing spring; a shank bone, symbolizing the sacrificed lamb whose blood identified the homes of the Jews in Egypt, and a roasted egg, symbolizing the sacrifice in the Temple. In addition, a bowl containing vinegar or salt water is placed on the table to symbolize the bitterness of slavery.

Before the holiday begins, it is traditional to spring clean the household to remove all traces of leaven. It is customary for the head of the household to search the house the night before the holiday and find some crusts of bread that have been deliberately left. They are securely wrapped up and burned the next morning.

Traditional foods for Passover include a great variety of dishes made with matzoh, including kugels, cakes and pancakes of various types. Dairy products are traditional during the holiday, although the main course at the seder is often a substantial turkey or roast.

Charoses

SERVES 2—4

This mixture of apples, nuts, wine and spices symbolizes the clay the Hebrews used to make the bricks that built the pyramids. It is served at Passover with the bitter herbs as a reminder of the time of slavery.

1 cup walnuts, shelled

2 dessert apples, peeled and cored

$\frac{1}{2}$ cup sweet red wine

1 teaspoon ground ginger

1 teaspoon cinnamon

2 tablespoons honey

Chop the walnuts and apples together and combine with the wine in a wooden mixing bowl. Add the ginger, cinnamon and honey. Toss well.

Matzoh Brei

SERVES 2

A traditional breakfast during Passover. It can be made sweet by omitting the salt and pepper and substituting sugar and cinnamon.

2 eggs
salt to taste
black pepper to taste
2 matzohs, crushed
boiling water
2 tablespoons butter

Beat the eggs in a bowl with the salt and pepper. Put the matzoh pieces into a small bowl and dampen them with the boiling water. Force the dampened matzohs through a sieve. Stir the sieved matzohs into the egg mixture.

♦ Melt the butter in a skillet. Pour the matzoh-egg mixture into the skillet and cook until lightly browned on the underside. Turn the matzoh brei over and cook on the other side. Serve immediately.

Chremsel

SERVES 4

There are innumerable variations of these matzoh meal pancakes. They can be made sweet or savory, as one large pancake or several small ones. This version makes a number of small sweet pancakes.

4 eggs, separated
½ cup matzoh meal
½ cup water
1 teaspoon salt
½ cup peanut oil

Beat the egg whites in a bowl until they are stiff.

♦ Beat the egg yolks in another bowl. Put the matzoh meal into a bowl and add the water, salt and beaten egg yolks. Stir and leave to stand for 5 minutes. Fold in the egg whites.

♦ Heat the peanut oil in a large heavy skillet until it is very hot. Drop tablespoons of the chremsel mixture into the oil and sauté until brown on the bottom. Turn and sauté until browned on the other side. Serve hot with sugar, soured cream and/or preserves.

Purim

Also called the Feast of Esther or the Feast of Lots, Purim is a joyous holiday observed on the fourteenth of Adar, in February or March. It celebrates the deliverance of the Jews of Persia by Esther and Mordecai from a plot for their extermination by the evil Haman. The story is told in the Book of Esther. The scroll, or megillah, is read aloud. The children in the audience jeer and hiss whenever Haman's name is read. A seudah, or Purim feast, is served that day. Purim is also a time for festivities and gifts of food.

Purim Soup

SERVES 6

Traditionally served on Purim in Eastern Europe, this soup has a slightly sweet flavor.

> 1 pound beef brisket, cubed
>
> 2 beef soup bones
>
> $4\frac{1}{2}$ cups water
>
> 1 cup tomato juice
>
> 2 leeks, white part only, julienned
>
> 6 cauliflower flowerettes
>
> 1 tablespoon salt
>
> 2 tablespoons sugar
>
> 1 teaspoon freshly ground black pepper
>
> 2 egg yolks, beaten

Put the beef, soup bones and water in a large, deep saucepan and bring to a boil. Cover and simmer for 90 minutes.

♦ Remove the soup bones and skim the surface of the soup. Add the tomato juice, leeks, cauliflower, salt, sugar and pepper. Bring to a boil, cover and simmer over a medium heat for 15 minutes.

♦ Put the egg yolks in a soup tureen. Remove the soup from the heat and slowly pour the soup over the egg yolks, stirring constantly. Serve hot.

Hamentaschen

MAKES ABOUT 75 HAMENTASCHEN

These filled pastries are traditional on Purim. As well as the traditional prune filling given here, Hamentaschen are often filled with either a prepared poppy-seed mixture called mohn *or with any sort of preserve.*

> 4 eggs
>
> 1 cup sugar
>
> $\frac{1}{2}$ cup vegetable oil
>
> 3 tablespoons lemon juice
>
> grated rind of 1 lemon
>
> 1 teaspoon pure vanilla extract
>
> 2 teaspoons baking powder
>
> 5 cups unbleached flour

For the filling:
3 cups prune butter lekvar
1 cup seedless raisins
1 cup chopped walnuts
grated rind of 1 lemon or orange
1 tablespoon vegetable oil

Beat the eggs in a mixing bowl. Gradually stir in the sugar until the mixture thickens and bubbles appear. Gradually mix in the oil, lemon juice, lemon rind and vanilla extract. Add the baking powder and, mixing continuously, add the flour until a stiff dough is formed. Turn the dough out on to a floured surface and knead, adding more flour if necessary, until a stiff, non-sticky dough is formed.

♦ To make the filling, combine the prune butter, raisins, walnuts, citrus rind and oil in a bowl. Mix well.

♦ Preheat the oven to 375°F. Roll out a small piece of the dough until thin.

♦ With a 1 inch pastry cutter, cut circles of dough. Place one teaspoon of the filling in the center of each dough. Pinch together 3 points on the circle tightly to make a triangle. Repeat with the remaining dough and filling.

♦ Place the hamentaschen on a greased baking sheet and bake for 20 minutes. Remove them from the oven and leave them to cool on the baking sheet for 15 minutes. Finish cooling them on wire racks.

Bean Cakes

SERVES 6

These Russian Bean Cakes are very popular at Purim.

1 cup cooked black-eye peas
1 tomato
1 onion
salt to taste
black pepper to taste
2 cups vegetable oil

Purée the black-eye peas in a blender or food processor until smooth, adding small amounts of cold water if needed. Put the purée into a mixing bowl.

♦ Purée the tomato and onion until smooth. Add to the black-eye peas. Season to taste with salt and pepper. Mix well.

♦ Heat the oil in a large heavy skillet until it is very hot. Drop teaspoons of the bean mixture into the skillet and sauté until brown on both sides. Drain on paper towels.

Chanuka

In Hebrew the word chanuka *means dedication. The holiday of
Chanuka, which begins on the twenty-fifth day of Kislev, December, is
also called the Feast of Dedication or the Feast of Lights. This eight-day
holiday celebrates the victory of the Maccabees over the Syrians in 165
BCE and the rededication of the Temple, which had been defiled by the
tyrant Antiochus.*

*Chanuka is celebrated by lighting candles every night in commemoration
of a miraculous flask of oil that burned for eight days instead of one
when the Temple was rededicated. The holiday is also traditionally
celebrated by giving children small gifts of money, called Chanuka gelt,
and by playing games with a top called a driedel. In terms of Jewish
history Chanuka is a recent holiday. In Western societies it has perhaps
taken on disproportionate importance, particularly in terms of
gift-giving, because of its proximity to Christmas.*

Potato Pancakes

SERVES 4—6

*This hearty dish, which has become a classic of Jewish cuisine around the world,
originated with the German-Austrian Jews. Although most cook books suggest that
the pancakes should be served with a choice of soured cream or apple sauce,
connoisseurs know that they should be eaten with both.*

*Potato pancakes are traditionally served on Chanuka. This is probably because the
oil they are cooked in is a reminder of the miraculous flask of oil that burned for eight
days and nights when the temple in Jerusalem was rededicated by the victorious Jews
in 165 BCE.*

12 large potatoes
4 eggs
$\frac{1}{2}$ cup finely chopped onion
$\frac{1}{2}$ cup flour
2 teaspoons salt
1 cup vegetable oil

Peel the potatoes and submerge them in a large bowl of cold water.

◆ In a large mixing bowl, beat the eggs and onion together. Gradually add the flour
and salt, beating constantly.

◆ Drain and pat dry the potatoes. Coarsely grate them and drain them well. Press to
remove as much moisture as possible. It is better to use the coarse side of a hand
grater than to use a blender or food processer, which make the potatoes too wet.

◆ Stir the grated potatoes into the onion-egg mixture until the mixture is evenly
blended. Form the mixture into flat pancakes about 4-5 inches in diameter and $\frac{1}{2}$
inch thick.

◆ Heat the vegetable oil in a heavy skillet over a moderate heat. When the oil is very
hot, reduce the heat slightly. Using a spatula, put the pancakes in the oil and sauté
until they are golden brown and the edges are crisp, about 2 minutes per side.

◆ Serve hot with soured cream, apple sauce, and/or preserves.

North African Chanuka Fish
SERVES 6

The Jews of North Africa have a distinct cuisine based on native foods. Any firm, white-fleshed fish can be used.

$\frac{1}{2}$ cup cooked rice

$\frac{1}{2}$ cup chopped almonds

4 tablespoons sugar

$\frac{1}{2}$ cup butter

$\frac{1}{2}$ teaspoon ground ginger

salt to taste

black pepper to taste

$\frac{1}{2}$ pound dates, pitted

6 pounds fish, cleaned

1 onion, sliced

1 tablespoon cinnamon

Preheat the oven to 350°F. Combine the rice, almonds, sugar, 2 tablespoons butter, ginger, salt and pepper in a mixing bowl. Mix well. Stuff the dates with the mixture and close the openings with toothpicks. Pack the cavity of the fish with the stuffed dates.

♦ Grease a large baking dish with the remaining butter. Put the fish in the dish and top with the onion slices. Bake until the fish flakes easily with a fork, about 25 to 30 minutes.

♦ Remove the dates from the fish and arrange the fish on a serving platter. Arrange the dates around the fish and dust with the cinnamon.

Sephardic Date Cakes
MAKES 16

Dates are a staple food in North Africa and the Middle East. These cookies or menana *are a traditional Sephardic treat on Chanuka.*

$\frac{3}{4}$ pound dates, pitted

$\frac{1}{2}$ pound butter

2 tablespoons sugar

2 cups flour

$\frac{1}{4}$ cup water

2 teaspoons orange juice

superfine sugar for dusting

Soak the dates in enough cold water to cover for 2 hours. Drain well and pat dry with paper towels. Finely chop the dates in a blender or food processor. Set aside.

♦ Preheat the oven to 350°F. Line a baking sheet with aluminum foil.

♦ Cream the butter and sugar together until they are fluffy. Gradually add the flour, water and orange juice. The dough will be quite soft.

♦ Shape the dough into 16 small balls. Make an indentation in each ball with your finger and fill it with $\frac{1}{2}$ teaspoon of the chopped dates. Close the indentation and gently shape each ball into a round, flat cake about 2 inches across.

♦ Place the cookies on the baking sheet and bake for 30 to 40 minutes, or until they are lightly browned. Leave them to cool and dust with superfine sugar.

Succoth

Also called the Feast of Tabernacles, Succoth falls on the fifteenth day of Tishre, in September or October. The holiday commemorates the period when the Israelites wandered in the Sinai wilderness and slept in booths, or sukkot. Succoth is also a harvest festival, as symbolized by the waving of the lulav — the palm frond — and the etrog — the citron. In ancient times, Succoth was one of the three pilgrimage festivals, holidays where it was the duty of all Israelites to attend services at the Temple in Jerusalem. The eighth day of Succoth is called Shemini Atzeret, or the Feast of the Conclusion. The day after that is called Simchat Torah, the day when the reading aloud of the Torah during the course of the preceding year has been completed, and a new reading begins.
The American holiday of Thanksgiving was modelled on Succoth by the Pilgrims as they gave thanks for their first successful harvest.

Date and Nut Pudding

SERVES 6—8

This dish comes from the Russian tradition, but has a Middle Eastern flavor.

> 2 cups dates, pitted and chopped
> 1 cup walnut halves
> $\frac{3}{4}$ cup flour
> $1\frac{1}{2}$ teaspoons baking powder
> $\frac{1}{2}$ teaspoon salt
> 3 eggs
> 1 tablespoon sugar
> whipped cream

Preheat the oven to 325°F. Grease a 9 inch square baking dish.
♦ In a bowl combine the dates, walnuts, flour, baking powder and salt.
♦ Beat the eggs with the sugar in a small bowl. Add to the date mixture and mix well. Pour the mixture into the baking dish and bake for 40 minutes.
♦ Serve warm with whipped cream.

Raisin Relish

MAKES $1\frac{1}{2}$ CUPS

This piquant, sweet-and-sour relish is typically Polish.

> 1 cup golden seedless raisins, chopped
> 1 scant tablespoon chopped ginger
> 2 garlic cloves, finely chopped
> $1\frac{1}{2}$ teaspoons sugar
> $\frac{1}{4}$ teaspoon mustard seeds
> $\frac{1}{4}$ teaspoon cayenne pepper
> $\frac{1}{4}$ teaspoon salt
> $\frac{1}{4}$ cup white wine vinegar

Put all the ingredients into a food processor or blender and process until finely chopped. Store in the refrigerator until ready for use.

Rosh Hashana

The Jewish New Year, or Rosh Hashana, is celebrated on the first and second days of Tishre, in September or October. It is a solemn holiday, for it marks the beginning of the Ten Days of Repentance that lead up to Yom Kippur, the Day of Atonement. The shofar or ram's horn is blown on Rosh Hashana as a reminder to the people of the need for improvement and atonement. Rosh Hashana is also a festive holiday, however, and large family dinners are customary. It is also traditional to serve sweet foods, such as apple slices dipped in honey, to symbolize the hope for a sweet year to come.

Mandelbrot

MAKES 40 SLICES

Literally 'almond bread', this Polish cookie keeps well when stored in a covered container.

3 eggs
$1\frac{1}{4}$ cups sugar
1 cup peanut oil
3 tablespoons orange juice
4 cups flour
4 teaspoons baking powder
$\frac{1}{4}$ teaspoon salt
$\frac{1}{4}$ cup candied fruit
1 cup chopped almonds

Preheat the oven to 350°F. Grease a 14 inch square baking sheet well.
♦ Beat the eggs in a bowl. Gradually beat in the sugar, then $\frac{1}{2}$ cup of the oil and the orange juice. Mix well.
♦ Combine the flour, baking powder, salt, candied fruit and almonds in a bowl. Add to the egg mixture and mix well to form a soft dough.
♦ With oiled hands shape the dough into 3 long flat bars the length of the baking sheet. Bake for 40 minutes or until lightly browned. Remove the baking sheet from the oven and cut the bars into diagonal slices about 1 inch wide with a sharp knife. Leave them to cool.

Teiglach

MAKES 30 COOKIES

These sticky, deep-fried cookies are served as a holiday treat in Russia.

> 4 cups flour
> 2 teaspoons baking powder
> 8 eggs
> 1 pound honey
> 1 cup sugar
> $1\frac{1}{2}$ teaspoon ground ginger
> $\frac{1}{2}$ cup chopped walnuts
> $\frac{1}{2}$ cup chopped candied fruit

In a large bowl combine the flour, baking powder and eggs. Mix well to form a stiff dough.

♦ Turn the dough out on to a floured surface and knead well. Roll the dough into strips $\frac{1}{2}$ inch wide. Cut the strips into pieces about 1 inch long.

♦ Heat the honey in a saucepan. Add the sugar and ginger and stir well. Bring the honey to a boil. Drop the dough pieces into the boiling honey in batches and cook, stirring frequently, until the teiglach rise to the surface. Put the teiglach on a serving platter and sprinkle with the walnuts and candied fruit.

Rogelach

MAKES 36 COOKIES

The dough for these cookies is quite rich. The cookies may burn slightly on the bottom, but this is an accepted part of the flavor.

> $\frac{1}{2}$ cup butter
> $\frac{1}{2}$ cup cream cheese
> $\frac{1}{2}$ cup soured cream
> $1\frac{1}{4}$ cups flour
> 1 cup chopped walnuts
> $\frac{1}{2}$ cup sugar
> 1 teaspoon cinnamon
> $\frac{1}{2}$ cup seedless dark raisins

Cream the butter and cream cheese together in a large mixing bowl. Mix in the soured cream. Add the flour and mix well. Divide the dough into two balls. Wrap each ball in plastic wrap and refrigerate overnight.

♦ Preheat the oven to 375°F.

♦ In a bowl combine the walnuts, sugar, cinnamon and raisins.

♦ Roll out the first dough ball on a floured surface into a circle about 16 inches in diameter. Cut the circle into 18 pie-shaped wedges. Sprinkle the circle with half the walnut mixture. Repeat with the second dough ball.

♦ Starting at the wide end, roll up each wedge tightly. Curve the rolls slightly and place them on a greased baking sheet. Bake for 20 minutes, or until lightly browned.

INDEX

(Numbers in *italics* refer to illustrations.)

CREDITS

The publishers would like to thank the following for permission to reproduce copyright photographs: Jacket: Hing/Norton; pp. 6, 11 and 12 QED/Ian Howes; p. 8 David Burch; pp. 13 (top left), 151 (bottom right) The Jewish Experience; pp. 55, 122 (bottom) Moira Clinch; pp. 86 (top), 207 The Jewish Museum, New York; pp. 121, 123 (top, bottom left) German Information Center, New York; p. 122 (top) Uta Hoffman; pp. 149, 150 (top), 151 (left) French Government Tourist Office; pp. 175, 177 (top left, bottom left) F. Ontañón; p. 177 (top right) Mexico Ministry of Tourism; pp. 193, 194 (top), 195 (top left, top right, bottom left) British Tourist Authority, New York; p. 195 (bottom right) New York Convention & Visitors Bureau

Food styling pp. 15 (bottom), 16, 94 (bottom), 95, 145 (top), 146, 147 (top left) Any Pasco; pp. 14 (top, bottom), 15 (top), 51 (bottom), 118 (top left) Lynn Lazin

Special props courtesy Bronstein-Baskin Foundation, Libby Baskin, Francis Glic, Miriam Levy

Food preparation Janine Norton and Edward Hing

Special thanks to Mr & Mrs Gilbert E. Rosenzweig and Mr & Mrs Martin Burstein for use of silver and ritual objects from their collections